DID I SAY THAT?

LESLIE B. FLYNN

*Though this book is designed for the reader's
personal enjoyment and profit, it is also intended
for group study. A Leader's Guide with Victor
Multiuse Transparency Masters is available from
your local bookstore or from the publisher.*

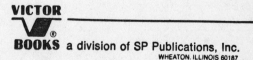

VICTOR
BOOKS® a division of SP Publications, Inc.
WHEATON. ILLINOIS 60187

Offices also in
Whitby, Ontario, Canada
Amersham-on-the-Hill, Bucks, England

Recommended Dewey Decimal Classification: 248
Suggested Subject Heading: CHRISTIAN WALK

Library of Congress Catalog Number: 85-062699
ISBN: 0-89693-253-2

VICTOR BOOKS
A division of SP Publications, Inc.
        Wheaton, Illinois 60187

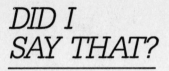

DID I
SAY THAT?

CONTENTS

Preface   7

1   The Idle Word   9

2   Blotting Out the Blot   21

3   A Keen Sense of Rumor   35

4   Examining Your Exclamations   47

5   Forked Lightning   59

6   Do You Needle People?   71

7   To Tell the Truth   83

8   Are You a Litterbug?   95

9   Patting Yourself on the Back   106

10   Songs at Midnight   117

11   Thermometer and Thermostat   129

12   Better Sweet Than Bittersweet   141

To my grandchildren:

Jeremy
Amber
Cori
Bobby
Jimmy
John Peter
Carolyn
Tara
Casie
Bobbi

and to any others that may yet arrive.

PREFACE

Bernard H. Goetz, who claimed self-defense in shooting four youths just before Christmas, 1984 in a New York City subway train, was acquitted of all charges except possession of an illegal weapon. But a second grand jury, called because of purported new evidence, indicted Goetz on four counts of attempted murder and other charges as well. Some close associates claimed Goetz talked too much about the incident after his acquittal by the first grand jury. Had he kept quiet and refrained from certain remarks, the case would never have been revived, they asserted.

How easily the tongue speaks unnecessarily, or spews out rumors, half-truths, and a host of evil words. Yet strangely, few treatises on moral philosophy give extended space to the subject of the tongue. Though Aristotle's *Nicomachean Ethics* presents no formal treatment on the theme, it does contain a few short paragraphs on buffoonery, wit, and boastfulness. Admittedly, many maxims have developed on the power of words such as: "A long tongue means a short life"; "Man is master of the unspoken word, which spoken, is master of him"; "A sharp tongue is the only tool that grows sharper with constant use." But extended discourses on the topic of the tongue do not seem to exist.

Even as amazing, few Christian authors or preachers seem to deal with the tongue. This omission, both secular and sacred, is significant. It reveals with what little import we regard the sins of speech. An angry word uttered in hot haste, an insidious insinuation, a thoughtlessly uttered swearword, and the passing

7

on of the latest morsel of choice gossip, we usually relegate to the oblivion of the inconsequential, even though we later may wish we had bitten our tongue off at the moment of utterance.

But with what serious regard the Bible considers slips of speech! Two of the Ten Commandments refer to the tongue, those forbidding taking God's name in vain and lying. The Book of Proverbs is packed with over a hundred warnings against unprincipled talk. Jesus joltingly warned, "Every idle word that men shall speak, they shall give account thereof in the day of judgment" (Matt. 12:36). Paul forbade corrupt conversation and advised speech seasoned with salt. Recognizing the deadly poison of the tongue, James devoted an entire chapter to its unruly nature. We may hold slips of the tongue of little import, but God regards them seriously.

Chapters in this book deal with swearing, criticism, gossip, contention, anger, lying, dirty talk, boastfulness, complaining, and suggest helps to overcome in these areas.

This is not a book on the tongues movement, but on the movement of the tongue.

ONE
THE IDLE WORD

President Reagan, testing the mike prior to a regular Saturday afternoon broadcast, spoke in jest about bombing Russia. Somehow a reporter got hold of this off-the-cuff remark, and perhaps unwisely published it. Before long the whole world knew what the President had said.

This reminds us of Jesus' statement that "whatsoever ye have spoken in darkness shall be heard in the light; and that which ye have spoken in the ear in closets shall be proclaimed upon the housetops" (Luke 12:3).

WHAT'S AN IDLE WORD?

When I was a student in Bible school, we often told jokes while standing around the breakfast table, waiting for the blessing. At some pause in the laughter, a good brother at our table who invariably was reading from his New Testament would look up and in a sepulchral voice intone, "Remember, brethren, 'Every idle word that men shall speak, they shall give account thereof in the day of judgment' '' (Matt. 12:36). This put a damper on our humor—until the next morning.

Does this text forbid joking, wit, and the pleasantries of social conversation? Just what is an "idle word"?

The word *idle* is a combination of a negative prefix and the noun *work,* literally *free from work, not working, thus idle.* One inactive element discovered by scientists was named after the Greek word for *idle*—argon. *Idle* appears about half a dozen times in the New Testament, but isn't always translated *idle.* "Faith without works is dead" (James 2:20) could read, "Faith without works is idle." Peter wanted believers to "neither be barren nor unfruitful in the knowledge of our Lord Jesus Christ" (2 Peter 1:8). "Barren" is the same word as *idle.* Coupled with *unfruitful,* it indicates the idea of unproductiveness.

So an idle word is one which hasn't been worked over, or thought through. Other translations speak of every *thoughtless* or *careless* word.

Jesus uttered His startling warning because the Pharisees had just spoken idly. The context goes back to Matthew 12:22 where Jesus, who had healed a blind, dumb, and demon-possessed man, was openly acclaimed as the promised Son of David (12:23). The envious Pharisees, who had to say something in the face of these claims, thoughtlessly suggested that Jesus' power came from the prince of demons.

Jesus easily disposed of this preposterous accusation by showing that if He were expelling demons by the prince of demons, then Satan's house was divided against itself. The only possible explanation for such a remark by the Pharisees was that they made it without thinking their words through. It was an idle charge, thrown out in the heat of controversy, on the principle that any stick is good enough to beat a dog with.

Examples of idle words abound in modern life. A man,

learning that another employee had just received a promotion, exclaims, "He knows how to butter up the boss—that's why he got promoted."

A lady, seeing a moving van with a new living-room set drive up to her neighbor's house, remarks, "She can't be a tither, or she couldn't afford that furniture."

Another lady, separated from her husband, granted the custody of her two children to her husband, realizing it would be the best arrangement for all concerned. But friends and relatives insisted on making thoughtless comments such as, "No decent mother would give her kids away," or "She probably wanted to be free to run around."

When a family leaves a church, members are heard to say, "They're so vacillating and unpredictable. They're spiritual tramps."

When a pastor loses some of his flock to another church, he may react, "That pastor is a sheep-stealer. He proselytes from other churches."

If in any of these cases the evaluation is true, then the words would not be idle. (We should keep in mind, as will be pointed out later, that other factors may render true words unacceptable and improper.) But if the utterer, because he was confronted with an uncomfortable situation, has just tossed out words without thinking them through, he has spoken idle words.

Herein lies the danger of talkativeness, and the virtue of silence. The tongue that wags a lot must find something to say, very often uttering unexamined words. A talkative tongue, if carried away, may boast, exaggerate, flatter, or give out half-truths, innuendos, whisperings, false rumors, and even slander. A talkative tongue, if angry, may introduce swearwords or make contentious, ungrounded charges. A talkative tongue, if inclined to jest without restraint, may include off-color stories in its repertoire. No wonder the Bible says, "Don't talk so much. You keep putting your foot in your mouth. Be sensible and turn off the flow!'' (Prov. 10:19, TLB)

Jesus' enemies tried to induce Him to speak about many things, hoping thus to trap Him in His speech. Because we are less likely to use thoughtless words if we speak less, James urges, ''Be swift to hear, slow to speak'' (James 1:19). Some secular proverbs suggest the same thought: ''Men are born with two eyes, but one tongue, in order that they should see twice as much as they say''; ''Many things are opened by mistake, but none so frequently as the mouth''; and from the Bible, ''He that hath knowledge spareth his words'' (Prov. 17:27).

Are humorous words idle words? Sometimes, but not always. Humor, properly used, is a gift from God. The biographies of most men of God reveal that they had their moments of bubbling laughter and merriment.

It has been well pointed out that we shall have to answer, not for wise words spoken in humor, but for foolish (careless, thoughtless) words spoken in earnestness.

WHAT'S SO SERIOUS ABOUT IDLE WORDS?

Why did Jesus regard idle words so seriously? Because of their implications Godward, selfward, and fellowmanward.

Godward—Idle words debase a wonderful gift from God. Of all earthly creations, man alone has the full gift of speech. Inanimate nature does not speak. Speech is more than a mere emitting of sounds like the crashing of thunder, the rippling of waves, or the whistling of wind. Speech and reason are closely allied. Speech is the expression of reason. Thinking is speaking within, while speaking is thinking out loud. Because lower creatures do not posssess reason or intelligence to any degree approximating that of humans, they cannot think discursively or go through the process of a syllogism.

Even parrots do not speak. A parrot parrots, oblivious to the meaning of what it is parroting. But God has given man both reason and a highly developed voice box which permits articulate speech to express what he is thinking. Only man has the physical apparatus which produces involved linguistic sounds. How dare we abuse this marvelous privilege by using it to utter idle words!

Introducing Thomas Edison at a banquet in the inventor's honor, the emcee listed his many inventions, dwelling at length on the talking machine. When Edison rose to his feet, he smiled, "I thank the gentleman for his kind remarks, but I must insist on one correction. It was God who invented the first talking machine. I only invented the first one that could be shut off!" To vitiate this amazing gift of speech makes us accountable for our careless words.

Selfward—Idle words disclose our true natures. An accent often betrays a person's geographical or national origin. Peter's Galilean accent gave him away the night he denied Christ. Bystanders taunted, "Surely thou also art one of them; for thy speech betrayeth thee" (Matt. 26:73).

The Gileadites, in combat, cornered the Ephraimites at the River Jordan. The Ephraimites claimed to be Gileadites. The Gileadites then asked the Ephraimites to say *shibboleth*, which meant *river*. The Ephraimites could not pronounce this word properly but said *sibboleth*. Betrayed by their speech, 42,000 Ephraimites were slain that day (Jud. 12:5-6).

When I came to school in Chicago from Canada in my late teens, I was amused by the many odd accents in the student body. I soon learned to distinguish people from New England, the South, and Brooklyn by the way they spoke. Likewise, they thought that I, a Canadian, spoke oddly. I pronounced the last letter of the alphabet *zed* instead of *zee*. I gave *house* and *about* a distinctive *oo* sound—*hoose* and *aboot*. I recall the bewilderment of the first church group I addressed in the U.S.A. when I asked them to look up the Book of *Sams*. Till they caught on that I was referring to *Psalms,* they thought I was a heretic, introducing an extra book into the sacred canon.

Just as accent indicates geographical origin, so speech exposes the condition of the heart. "You can judge the wheels a person has in his head by the spokes that come out of his mouth." The Arabs say, "The tongue's greatest storehouse is the heart." Spurgeon put it, "What lies in the well of the heart will come up in the bucket of speech." Or as the Master tersely said just before His warning against idle words, "Out of the abundance of the heart the mouth speaketh" (Matt. 12:34). A scientist has developed a machine called the Voiceprinter, which he claims can identify a human voice as reliably as fingerprints. Your voice gives you away.

Some argue that lenience must be shown those uttering idle words in highly emotional and off-guard moments. But Jesus would remind us that it's just when we are off guard that we reveal what's down deep within. In prepared speeches we exercise care as to our choices of words, but words spoken in unguarded moments reflect the true conditions of our hearts.

Justin said, "By examining the tongue of a patient, the physician finds out the diseases of the body, and the philosopher the diseases of the mind." Similarly, the Great Physician knows that the diseases of the spirit are disclosed by the tongue.

What is uppermost in the heart is bound to spew forth in conversation. A murmuring tongue indicates a complaining heart. A critical tongue reveals a judging heart. A swearing tongue springs from a sacrilegious heart. A filthy tongue flows from a dirty heart. Since what we say shows what kind of person we really are, idle words are serious. Our idle speech is enough to send every one of us to a lost eternity. Jesus said, "For by thy words thou shalt be justified, and by thy words thou shalt be condemned" (Matt. 12:37).

Manward—Idle words do damage to others. The tongue is a little thing but, like a germ, can do much damage: it can kindle a fire, defile a whole body, set on fire the course of nature, cause strife, confusion, and every evil work (James 3:5-16).

A few years ago some high school students in an Indiana town started a rumor that a nearby farmer kept a coffin in his living room, containing the corpse of a woman, which he guarded from curious eyes with a shotgun. As the rumor grew, crowds of inquisitive students began swarming over the property of this man. Not understanding the reason for the invasion every evening after dark, he ordered everyone off his property, backing up his order with a shotgun. The gun, of course, added impetus to the rumor, bringing more onlookers. Police, deluged with calls, declared after several investigations that there was no foundation to the tale. Despite police denials, crowds continued to gather nightly in front of his house. The firecracker blasts and raucous laughter preyed upon him until in desperation he fired his shotgun into his mouth. A thoughtless rumor drove him to suicide.

What havoc the tongue has wreaked. It has broken homes, divided families, sent innocent men to prison, crushed hearts, blasted churches, and even sent some to an early grave.

> The man who with the breath lent him by heaven
>   Speaks words that soil the whiteness of a life
> Is but a murderer, for death is given
>   As surely by the tongue as by the knife.
> —Author unknown

ACCOUNTABILITY FOR IDLE WORDS
Recording machines are a modern invention, but God has been recording since Creation. Job's prayer has long been answered,

"Oh that my words were now written! Oh that they were printed in a book!" (Job 19:23) A scientific laboratory in Princeton, New Jersey perfected a 12-inch vinyl disc, capable of storing the entire *Encyclopaedia Britannica*. Because a laser beam does the recording, this disc has a capacity 100 times greater than magnetic tape. Doubtless more efficient and compact methods of recording will yet be devised. The seer of Revelation visualized the judgment day when "the books were opened" which will contain among other items all our idle words (Rev. 20:12).

A person who hears his voice played back on a recording device for the first time often fails to recognize it. It would be even more shocking to hear our words played back for a whole week. In the early presentations of *Sermons from Science*, Dr. Irwin Moon often walked through the audience, asking people to quote verses into his hand-held microphone. Understandably nervous, a person sometimes stammered or misquoted. Then Dr. Moon would play back the recording before the entire audience. What embarrassment for the person who had made a mistake, when his stammering and error came back word for word, syllable for syllable, exactly as originally spoken. How he wished it could be erased. Would we like to hear our words of just one day played back for others to hear?

It is estimated that each of us on the average speaks enough words every day to fill at least 20 typewritten pages. This minimum adds up to three books of 200 pages each month, 36 books a year, and 1,800 books in a lifetime of 50 speaking years. What a library!

> If all that we say
> In a single day,
> With never a word left out,
> Were printed each night
> In clear black and white,

'Twould prove odd reading, no doubt.
And then just suppose
'Ere one's eyes he could close,
He must read the day's record through.
Then wouldn't one sigh.
And wouldn't one try
A great deal less talking to do?
And I more than half think
That many a kink
Would be smoothed in life's tangled thread,
If one-half that we say
In a single day
Were left forever unsaid.
                                        —Author unknown

In the early years of phonographs a lady, reputed to have the sharpest ears in the business, spent several hours every working day in a secluded room, doing nothing but listening to first platters of master records. If she okayed a record, it was released to the public. But if she caught any dent, tick, or swish, the master platter had to be repaired or rerecorded. Her daily concert in solitary confinement consisted of about 50 records. In 20 years she tested more than 70,000 records. Incidentally, she had no phonograph in her home.

She was the one who heard that additional line or two after the number was through, but before the recording machine had stopped cutting. Often she heard the recording artist, thinking he was "off the cutter," let loose in self-adulation, "Boy, was I good!" Sometimes she heard the bang of an angry or recklessly jubilant bandleader's baton against the recording mike. Once she caught Toscanini expressing an expert opinon on his wind section. These additions always had to be edited off the record.

God above has a record of every word we have ever said.

Though in interviews with journalists people often say, "This isn't for publication," with God there is nothing "off the record." Someday every word spoken in the dark will be proclaimed on the housetop. Nixon never dreamed his Watergate tapes would someday be made public. How often behind-the-scene remarks, or comments in the heat of political activity, bring embarrassment, such as President Reagan's joking threat to bomb Russia, or Geraldine Ferraro's skepticism as to the reality of the President's religion.

A radio celebrity, finishing his children's program, and thinking the mike was turned off, remarked, "That ought to hold the little so-and-so's." His slur went out over the air waves with resultant furor and the loss of his job. God's mike is never off.

Ex-wiretapper Jim Vaus once wired several spots in a church where he was scheduled to hold a series of meetings. At the close of the first service he announced that he had recorded the conversations of several people at scattered places around the auditorium and would play them back the next night. The minute the service ended several men approached Vaus, eagerly offering to buy those tapes. Later Vaus discovered he had forgotten to turn the switch on.

A group of husbands had a jovial time laughing and chatting in the living room after a dinner party, while their wives were finishing up the dishes in the kitchen. One man of high moral character who was known to tell only clean jokes, related a dirty story that brought an uproarious response, as well as looks of amazement from some who knew his usually high standards. When the ladies joined the men in the living room, the host announced, "I've a surprise for you. Last week I bought a tape recorder, and I've had it on while you were in the kitchen. I thought you might like to hear what the men were talking about."

The man who had told the off-color story began to turn white.

Then his face seemed to get red with anticipated embarrassment. The recorder was switched on. Back came the conversation, every word, every tone, every inflection, just as the men had uttered them minutes before. As it neared the joke, the man began to squirm in his chair. Perspiration stood out on his forehead. He looked as if he wished the floor would open up and swallow him.

Then out came his voice, telling the story just as he had related it. It was about to reach the punch line that made it a dirty story. Suddenly the doorbell rang. Several exclaimed loudly, "There's someone at the door!" Their voices blotted out the conclusion of his story. The man gave a sigh of relief, relaxed in his chair, and with a smile wiped the perspiration from his forehead.

Thank God that we can have the penalty of our idle words forgiven by the blood of Christ. But as believers we must someday appear before the Judgment Seat of Christ to give an account of the words spoken by our tongues, as well as of the deeds done in our bodies. Unless we face up to our speech now, we will have to account for it in the judgment day.

Ann Landers told of a clerk in an exclusive ladies' dress shop who after a fashion show discovered that a pair of lovely earrings was missing. The clerk assumed that the customer who tried them on last had taken them. She repeated the story to several friends. A week later, while cleaning out her closet, the clerk found the earrings in a pocket of one of her dresses. She told Ann Landers that she would like to forget the whole episode, but that guilt kept gnawing relentlessly at her insides. The clerk wondered how she could make amends without looking foolish. Ann Landers told her to go to each and every person to whom she had told the story and explain that the earrings had turned up in a forgotten pocket and say, "I'm ashamed of myself." Ann Landers commented that the clerk would not look foolish, but rather like a person who had the courage to admit she was mistaken and the decency to clear the name of an innocent victim.

Paul wrote to believers, "If we would judge ourselves, we should not be judged" (1 Cor. 11:31).

We need to pray, "Set a watch, O Lord, before my mouth; keep the door of my lips" (Ps. 141:3).

TWO
BLOTTING OUT
THE BLOT

In an article on Secretary of State George P. Schultz, correspondent James Reston credits the secretary's so-far-successful performance in office partly to his quiet and reflective way of answering questions. Says Reston, "He doesn't take implied criticism personally or indulge in personal criticism himself" (*New York Times*, 3/25/83).

How easy it is to criticize. A lecturer once held up before an audience a large surface of pure white marred by one tiny blot. "What do you see?" he asked. "A blot," was the almost unanimous reply. Practically everyone ignored the white background.

How like human nature! We are quick to see the defects in others while overlooking their good qualities.

Jesus warned against the practice of always seeing the blot in the other fellow. He said, "Judge not, that ye be not judged" (Matt. 7:1).

WHAT KIND OF CRITICISM IS FORBIDDEN?

This command does not mean that civil courts should be abolished, or that evil must be tolerated, for there are occasions when blots must be seen and judged. For instance, we are ordered to "mark" those who cause divisions in our midst (Rom. 16:17). We are to choose as church officers those who meet certain criteria (1 Tim. 3:1-13). Paul told the Corinthian church to expel a fellow-member who was guilty of incest.

Christian, in *Pilgrim's Progress,* was perfectly justified in criticizing Talkative for his hypocrisy. The ability to take constructive criticism indicates one's level of spiritual maturity. "Reprove not a scorner, lest he hate thee; rebuke a wise man, and he will love thee" (Prov. 9:8).

Jesus' command prohibits the censorious spirit which reaches hasty conclusions or impugns the motives of others without sufficient foundation to make a judgment. Some persons seem to be born in the objective case—objecting to this, questioning that, accusing here, criticizing there. The only mental exercise some people take is jumping at conclusions, a dangerous practice, as this doggerel suggests:

> There was a dog named August,
> He was always jumping at conclusions;
> One day he jumped at the conclusion of a mule,
> That was the last day of August.
> —Author unknown

How easy to draw false conclusions from hasty premises. A child seeing a red apple for the first time may conclude that all apples are red. A man may take a five-day journey through Russia, return to America, and write a book on Russia. Some of his judgments will likely be false.

Judging often impugns the motives of others. "The reason he

gave such a nice check to the church is that he wanted to reduce his income tax,'' criticizes someone. The mere reporting of someone else's judgment may indicate that you subscribe to it. You are criticizing indirectly. How often the passing on of an opinion is subtle criticism.

Scripture contains examples of jumping at false judgments and of picking out flaws. Aaron and Miriam criticized their brother Moses: "Hath the Lord indeed spoken only by Moses?" (Num. 12:2) The Lord's anger was kindled against Aaron and Miriam. Miriam was stricken with leprosy for seven days, for she was guilty of evil-speaking against her brother, whom she had watched over when he was a baby in the ark in the bulrushes. Tragically, loved ones are a frequent target of our unkind judgment.

> One great truth in life I've found,
>   While journeying to the West;
> The only folks we really wound
>   Are those we love the best.
>
> We flatter those we scarcely know,
>   We please the fleeting guest,
> And deal full many a thoughtless blow
>   To those we love the best.
>   —Ella Wheeler Wilcox

When David came down to bring food to his brothers arrayed in battle against the Philistines, he saw Goliath strutting forth to defy the Israelites and wondered why no one of the army of the Lord had gone to meet him in battle. But David's brothers falsely charged the lad with coming down in pride to see the battle (1 Sam. 17:28).

When the King of Ammon died, King David sent messengers

to convey expressions of sympathy to the late monarch's son, Hanun. But Hanun falsely concluded that the messengers had come to spy out and overthrow his kingdom, not to console. So he had David's messengers shaved and partially disrobed. David, learning of this humiliating treatment, was incensed and slew thousands of Ammonites in battle (2 Sam. 10).

Paul was once accused of desecrating the temple in Jerusalem. He had been spotted on the streets of the city in company with some Gentiles. His enemies wrongly inferred that he had brought one of them into the temple. Paul was beaten and almost killed (Acts 21:27-32).

Secular life, as well as the Scriptures, abound with examples of jumping at conclusions. Six-year-old Steve had picked up some swearwords, which caused his mother much anguish. One day he was invited to a playmate's birthday party. His mother's final word of warning as he went out was, "Stephen, I've asked them to send you straight home the minute you use a bad word."

Fifteen minutes later Steve walked in the door. His furious mother ordered him to bed, ignoring his attempts to explain. Later his mellowing mother went upstairs to see how he was taking it. Sitting at his bedside, she asked, "Tell me honestly, Steve, just why you were sent home. What swearword did you say?"

Little Steve, humiliated and still angry, replied, "I didn't say nuttin'. That party ain't till tomorrow!"

A lady invited several friends to a mushroom steak dinner. When her maid opened the can of mushrooms, she discovered a slight scum on the top. Since the guests were expected at any moment, the lady suggested, "Give the dog a little, and if he eats it, it's probably all right." The dog licked it and begged for more, so the dinner was completed.

After the main course, the maid came in to serve the dessert. But her face was ashen white. She whispered, "Ma'am, the dog's dead.'' There was only one thing to do. Sometime later the guests were reclining after the doctor left, in various stages of recovery from the use of a stomach pump. When the maid entered again, the lady asked, "Where's the poor dog now?"

Came the reply, "Out on the front steps, where he fell after the car hit him."

We should be careful not to create false impressions. The captain of a whaling ship once wrote in his log, "Mate got drunk today." When the mate sobered up, he saw the entry and knew the owner would fire him when they made port. So he begged the captain to strike it out, promising never to touch another drop. But the captain refused, "Anything once written in the log stays there." A few days later the mate was keeping the log. At the bottom of the page he wrote in large letters, "Captain was sober today."

The book *Mutiny on the Bounty* describes a trial of mutineers, in England. The most damaging evidence against a sailor by the name of Byam was Captain Bligh's testimony, who swore that the night before the mutiny he had heard Byam say to Fletcher Christian, the leader of the uprising, "You may count on me, sir." Byam was sentenced to death chiefly on this statement, since the witnesses who could prove his statement had a different meaning had died. However, one surviving witness, away on a voyage during the trial, returned to give sworn testimony that Byam's words had no connection with the mutiny but were rather a promise to Fletcher Christian to send his father a message if he failed to reach England. This resulted in Byam's freedom. Much misunderstanding has resulted from making judgments on remarks of which we have only a passing acquaintance.

A couple adopted a little boy from an orphanage. All were happy until one morning when some candies, kept by the couple in a bag on a table near the head of their bed, were missing.

Neither threat nor promise could extract a confession of guilt from the boy, so silently and sadly they drove to the orphanage and left him. That night they could not sleep. Suddenly, in the stillness, they were startled by the rustling of the paper bag containing the candy. Flicking on the light, they discovered a mouse was the thief. Long before dawn they sped away to bring the happy child home again.

THE DANGER OF CRITICISM
Unnecessary judging can be destructive. Like idle words, it has damaging implications Godward, selfward, and manward.

Judging assumes the prerogatives of God. An old Broadway play involved a deaf man who lived in an apartment high above Central Park in New York City. Using powerful binoculars, he read the lips of people seated on park benches far below. To those with problems he sent a servant with word that help was on its way. When asked the source of this help, the servant would reply, "It comes from the man who plays God."

When we judge the motives of men, we are claiming presumptuously for ourselves an insight that no human possesses—the ability to read the minds and purposes of others. Only God knows our thought lives, and only God is our Judge. When a person gives a large contribution, we have no right to say, "He's trying to lower his income tax." If we do, we are indirectly claiming, "I know as much as God knows about this. I can read his motives."

God's Word asks, "Why dost thou judge thy brother? . . . For we shall all stand before the Judgment Seat of Christ. . . . Let us not therefore judge one another any more" (Rom. 14:10, 13).

"Grudge not one against another, brethren, lest ye be condemned: behold, the Judge standeth before the door" (James 5:9).

We show ourselves candidates for judging. A young man who thought too highly of himself was standing in front of a taxidermist's store. In the window was an owl which had attracted many a sightseer. Anxious to display his knowledge, he said pompously, "If I couldn't stuff an owl better than that, I'd quit the business. The head isn't right. The pose of the body isn't right. The feet are not placed right." Just then the owl turned his head and winked at him. The crowd laughed, and the critic moved on.

When a VIP publicly insulted a reporter, a bystander remarked, "Mr. VIP may not realize it, but he has told us a lot more about himself than about Mr. Reporter."

A woman standing before an old masterpiece began to make a slighting comment. A man close by said, "Madam, that painting is no longer on trial—you are!"

A censorious spirit usually indicates feelings of inferiority, and is an expedient for raising self-importance and self-esteem. When we feel below a person, fallen human nature often wants to drag him down. Judging another shows we are on a lower level and in need of improvement. A negative self-image tends to run others down to boost its own ego. Criticism gives at the cheapest rate the feeling of equality or superiority.

> I hate the guys
> Who minimize and criticize
> The other guys
> Whose enterprise
> Has made them rise
> Above the guys who criticize.

In constantly dwelling on the flaws of others there looms the danger of self-complacency. As a Pharisee said, "God, I thank Thee that I am not as other men are" (Luke 18:11).

Also, judging others foreshadows a more dreadful judgment to come. Those who spoke against Moses—Korah and 250 others—were swallowed up by the yawning earth (Num. 16).

We injure others and our own testimony. Someone said, "The hammer is the only knocker that does any good." A young man, invited by a Christian friend to attend a Gospel service, accepted Christ as His Saviour. On the way home from the meeting the young men saw a couple of Christian ladies who had been present at the service. "How did you like the message?" asked the young men. Thereupon the ladies passed off a harsh criticism of the preacher. The young man who had made a profession of faith that night was startled by their remark and since then has seldom darkened the door of a church.

At Sunday dinner roast beef makes a good dish. But "roast preacher" is undesirable. If we want our children and friends to respect the preacher, we had better not find fault with him in their hearing. I thank God for the memory of parents who never discussed church trouble in my presence as I was growing up. Many children have been turned away from the Gospel by free and easy criticism of the preacher over the dinner table at home. Neither should we serve "roast Sunday School teacher," "roast soloist," or "roast organist." We cannot build up the Lord's work while tearing down His workers.

HOW TO OVERCOME THE CRITICAL TONGUE

Constructive criticism has its rightful place, but much criticism is destructive. A man once criticized another for his method of giving out tracts. "How do *you* do it?" asked the tract distributor.

"Er . . .ah . . . I don't," came the embarrassed critic's reply.

The personal worker retorted, "I like the way I do it better than the way you don't."

The spirit of censoriousness should be defeated. Here are suggestions to help overcome it.

We ourselves have faults subject to honest criticism. A man complained to his landlord about the noisy tenants above him who often stamped on the floor and shouted until after midnight. But then he added, "I guess they really don't bother me too much, for I usually stay up and practice the tuba until about that time every night anyway."

All of us have flaws which could provide legitimate grounds for criticism by others. Jesus said, "He that is without sin among you, let him first cast a stone at her" (John 8:7).

But it's far easier to see faults in others than in ourselves. We more quickly see a smudge on someone else's face than on our own. Little faults in others loom large in our vision, while large faults in ourselves appear little. A Quaker once said to his wife, "Everybody in this world is a bit queer except thee and me, and sometimes I think thee a bit queer."

> Faults in others I can see;
> But praise the Lord, there's none in me.
> —Author unknown

The Scottish poet Burns had some wise words,

> Oh wad some Power the giftie gie us
> To see oursels as others see us!

If we did see ourselves as others see us, we might be more inclined to say with a character in Shakespeare's *As You Like It*, "I will chide no brother in the world but myself, against whom I know most faults."

Strange as it may seem, we often judge others for the identical faults we possess. Jesus spoke of a man with a beam in his eye judging another who had a mote in his eye. Reduced to language which emphasizes the irony of the scene, Jesus was saying, "Here's a fellow with a tree trunk protruding from his eye criticizing another who has a sliver in his eye. First cast the tree trunk out of your eye. Then you'll see clearly to get the sliver out of the other fellow's eye."

The 10 disciples who so vehemently criticized James and John, whose mother had asked for the places of honor for her sons in the coming kingdom, wanted the same places for themselves.

A missionary on a furlough speaking engagement was given hospitality in a home one Sunday afternoon. In his room he used his portable typewriter to catch up on correspondence. The lady of the house rebuked him for using a typewriter on Sunday. An hour later, coming down into the living room, the missionary discovered the lady answering her correspondence with pen and ink.

A mother told her little girl not to exaggerate. "I've told you a million times not to exaggerate," she added.

A little boy exclaimed angrily to his big brother, "You're mean and selfish. You took the last apple, and I wanted it!"

A lady was showing a friend her neighbor's wash through her back window. "Our neighbor isn't very clean. Look at those streaks on her wash."

Replied her friend, "Those aren't on your neighbor's wash. They're on your window."

Your neighbor's wash looks much better when your windows are clean! So before flaring up at anyone else's faults, count to 10—10 faults of your own.

> There is so much good in the worst of us,
> And so much bad in the best of us,

That it ill behooves the best of us,
To talk about the rest of us.
—Author unknown

*The same pitfalls are possible to us under similar circum-
stances.* Perhaps someday you too might be guilty of the same
fault, given similar circumstances. Hence the advice, "Brethen,
if a man be overtaken in a fault, ye which are spiritual restore
such an one in the spirit of meekness; considering thyself, lest
thou also be tempted" (Gal. 6:1).

When you cannot understand how others could be guilty of
such blunders, remember that they possibly cannot comprehend
how you do the things you do. However, if you were in their
shoes and a product of the same background, you might easily
have been guilty of their faults. Years ago it was the custom of
some Indian tribes to appoint judges who traveled a circuit of
villages to try cases. Every judge was required to walk in the
forest alone, and pray this prayer, "O great Spirit, Maker of
men, forbid that I judge any man until I have walked for two
moons in his moccasins."

Pray don't find fault with the man who limps,
    Or stumbles along the road,
Unless you have worn the shoes he wears
    Or struggled beneath his load.
There may be tacks in his shoes that hurt,
    Though hidden away from view,
Or the burdens he bears, placed on your back,
    Might cause you to stumble too.
—Author unknown

Play the game of Christian cancellation. Two boys were
speaking of another lad. "He's so slow in baseball," said one.

"Yes," replied the other, "but he always plays fair."

"But he's so stupid at school," retorted the first.

"Yes," came the defense, "but he always studies hard."

Every unkind word spoken by the first boy was canceled by the second one. Let's try to think of the good points of another as well as the bad. When someone speaks of a blot, point out the white background.

A new employee in an insurance company's records department, where she knew she was not adjusting well, was called to the boss's office. As he leafed through papers which she was sure listed her faults and failures, he smiled, "Your supervisor tells me you get along very well with people, I think you could be valuable to us in the personnel department. How would you like to try it there?" She left the office singing, because he had concentrated on her strong point instead of dwelling on her obvious shortcomings.

Benjamin Franklin had an amusing way of determining which men possessed character suitable for companionshp. He introduced them to a close friend who had "a handsome leg and a deformed leg." If a stranger later spoke mainly of the deformed leg, and did not notice the handsome leg, that was enough to make Franklin have no further acquaintance with him. Ben advised critical, querulous, unhappy people, if they wished to be respected and loved by others, and happy in themselves, to stop looking at the "ugly" leg.

John Wesley and a preacher friend of plain manners once were invited to dinner where the host's daughter, noted for her beauty, had been profoundly impressed by Wesley's preaching. During a pause in the meal Wesley's friend took hold of the young lady's hand and lifting it, called attention to the sparkling rings she wore. "What do you think of this, sir, for a Methodist hand?"

The girl turned crimson. Wesley likewise was embarrassed, for his aversion to jewelry was well known. With a quiet, benevolent smile, he simply said, "The hand is very beautiful."

The young lady appeared at the evening service without her jewels and became a strong Christian.

We may not know all the facts. A man in a Pullman car on a train traveling through Texas couldn't sleep because of a bawling baby in the care of its father. The man called out, "Why don't you take that baby to its mother, so the rest of us can get some sleep?"

"Friend," replied the father, "I wish I could. But my wife, the baby's mother, died yesterday. Her body is in the baggage car ahead, and we're taking her back to her old home for burial."

We know so few of the facts about our fellowmen. Perhaps business isn't good, health is poor, a wife or husband isn't congenial, or a job has just been lost. If we had a full explanation, we would be sorry we judged. We do not have to give account of our neighbor's conduct at the throne of God. Everyone shall give account of himself, not of his neighbor.

The task of a judge or jury is seldom easy, even after the evidence has been presented. Human judgment is fallible. A newspaper once printed the pictures of the nine members of the Supreme Court without their names. They mixed these pictures with those of nine convicted murderers, again omitting names. The newspaper asked its readers to pick out which were which. People could not tell.

Interviewed by Barbara Walters, Mamie Eisenhower was asked if the rumors about her alcoholism were true. Mrs. Eisenhower answered that her problem was not the bottle, but loss of balance that made her bump into things. "I have what they call a carotid sinus. Your vein presses on your inner ear. I'm black and blue from walking around in my own house." Asked if the rumor upset her, she smiled and said, "I knew it wasn't true" (*Newsweek*).

A lady boarding a streetcar asked the conductor to let her off at a certain corner. He forgot till the car was two blocks past that corner. As she alighted, she gave the conductor a violent tongue lashing. He answered not a word. A passenger standing near asked him how he could take such a flow of abuse without retaliation. He replied, "It's true I was to blame for forgetting the corner, but that lady doesn't know that I have a sick wife at home—so sick she needs both day and night nurses. I have a day nurse there while I work, but I cannot afford a night nurse. So I've been staying up with her all night for the last two nights. I've worked every day because I need the money to pay the day nurse. So I haven't had a wink of sleep the last two days or nights. That's why my memory isn't working so well. The lady doesn't know these things."

The habit of constantly criticizing violates Scripture and dissipates spiritual vitality. John Wesley said, "Methodists are to be governed by the following rule—not to mention the fault of an absent person, in particular of ministers or of those in authority."

A person who claims to be spiritual and bridles not his tongue is deceived (James 1:26). But "a word fitly spoken is like apples of gold in pictures of silver" (Prov. 25:11).

THREE

A KEEN SENSE
OF RUMOR

The Lansman—Milam petition, RM 2493, filed with the Federal Communications Commission in 1974, was aimed at restricting the access of religious organizations to FM educational channels. Perceiving this as a threat to all religious broadcasting, the aroused American public flooded the FCC with letters.

By the time the petition was unanimously rejected in August, 1975, the FCC had received almost 1 million pieces of mail supporting religious stations. But despite the wide publicity given the FCC decision, a rumor still persists, 10 years later, that Madalyn Murray O'Hair is behind petition RM 2493 and wants to ban all religious programs from the airways. Form letters opposing RM 2493 reappear periodically in churches across the country, setting off new waves of mail. This bogus rumor has generated a volume of over 17 million letters, costing American taxpayers over a quarter million dollars as well as consuming thousands of man-hours in handling these petitions in Congressional and FCC offices, and wasting more than 3 million dollars in stamps. Over a million letters came in during 1984.

RUMORS

Another rumor that keeps cropping up concerns a "supposed" pornographic film featuring Jesus in a suggestive relationship with Mary Magdalene. Reportedly, a Swedish film company purchased rights to an unpublished novel, *The Many Faces of Christ,* in 1976, and planned to make a pornographic movie from it, but never did produce the film. When the rumor resurfaced in late 1983 with the claim that a movie portraying Jesus as "a swinging homosexual" was being distributed by an Illinois firm, the Illinois Attorney General's office was inundated with 170,000 letters of protest and 20 phone calls per day during the next 12 months.

When Dr. Stephen Olford was out of the U.S.A., holding meetings in England a few years ago, a rumor circulated that he had been murdered at Calvary Baptist Church in New York City where he had been pastor from 1959-1973. The National Association of Evangelicals, with whom Olford was then associated, received calls of condolence from all over the country at their Wheaton, Illinois headquarters. The report was refuted by Encounter Ministries, Inc., the organization Olford founded and leads.

Rumors revolving around shopping malls are widespread. Since the 1960s, with changes in location and minor details, the story has made the rounds concerning a woman shopper who suddenly realizes her little girl is missing. After a frantic search the daughter is found in a fitting room, dressed in boy's clothes and her long hair cut short.

Another floater involves a little old lady who tells shoppers she is sick and needs a ride home. "She" turns out to be a man in disguise who during the ride wields an ax. All officials can do is to tell people these stories are false and wait for the rumors to die down. Fortunately for the police, such rumors are short-lived in any given locality.

GOSSIP

Though similar in some respects, rumor and gossip should not be confused. A rumor is structured around unauthenticated information, and is usually untrue and unsubstantiated. Gossip, small talk about personal, confidential, behind-the-scenes, intimate, personal matters, may or may not be true. The material is usually entertaining, sometimes sensational. Gossiping is such a national pastime. We may listen to gossip in our circle of friends, tune in to radio and TV gossip programs, and read gossip columns. For several popular magazines gossip is big business. But even if a juicy morsel is true, this does not make it a legitimate object of conversation.

However, in all fairness, it must be pointed out that in its pure, innocent, and positive form gossip is basically news. Thus to a certain extent gossiping is normal and permissible. Psychologists tell us that except when indulged in excessively or vindicatively, gossip may be good for us. Letting off steam through harmless gossip may provide a therapeutic value to the gossiper. One psychologist said the happiest and best-adjusted people enjoy the exchange of gossip, but do so in moderation. The least happy and most poorly adjusted either carry the practice to the extreme, or don't gossip at all. After all, gossip in the good sense springs from an interest in others, in their activities, and in the news of community and world. Oscar Wilde said that all history was gossip.

Furthermore, there are times when duty demands gossip in order to protect the common good. For example, if a man were known to sit home every Saturday night and become intoxicated, nothing would be gained by tattling that publicly. But if that man were known to become intoxicated and then drive through busy intersections every Saturday night, this should be reported to some responsible authority.

RUMOR AND GOSSIP TEND TO PLAY FAST AND LOOSE WITH THE FACTS

A lady known for her gossiping came to the church altar at the end of a service, "Pastor, I'd like to place my tongue on the altar."

He replied, "I'd like to help you, but the altar is only 15 feet long."

Though that retort exaggerated the size of her tongue, we cannot overestimate the lengths to which a rumor can grow. A professor of sociology at Northeastern University decided to plant a rumor, to study its path of progress. He passed out flyers inviting people to an interfaith wedding. But he purposely passed them out the day after the purported wedding. No wedding really took place, and the names of the bride and groom were fictitious. A week later the psychologist conducted a survey to see how many people had heard about the wedding. Over half the students questioned had heard about the wedding, and startlingly, 12 percent of those surveyed told him they had been at the ceremony in person. What's more, some even described the bride's dress and the black limousine they saw whisk the couple off on the first leg of their Jamaican honeymoon.

How easily different people, hearing the very same thing, deduce widely differing meanings. Three men tried to hear a conversation between a man and his wife in the next room, and then were asked to guess the subject. The first man said they were talking about the zoo, because he had heard the words "trained deer." The second said it was about traveling, because he had heard, "Find out about the train, Dear." The third claimed the subject was music, for he had heard, "trained ear." The lady had simply asked her husband if it had rained here last night.

Very often in passing on a true account we add a little embellishment to make it a "better" story, filling in details of which we have no knowledge. A man said, "I like the parrot. It's the only creature gifted with the power of speech that is content to repeat just what it hears without trying to make a good story out of it." How paradoxical—a dumb creature tells exactly what it hears while enlightened, gifted creatures add to what they hear. The parrot doesn't have a keen sense of rumor. (Perhaps it was more than a typographical error when a newspaper reported that a prominent lady socialite was in the local hospital for the removal of a rumor.)

Another factor that makes for the spread of rumor and gossip, whether accurate or embellished, is that we never know who may overhear our conversation. Once when my wife picked up the phone to make a call, because of crossed wires she overheard a couple soon to be married engaged in a heated argument. She suggested I give them extra counseling before performing the wedding.

Another time my wife and a teacher friend were sitting in a shopping mall, discussing the qualifications of a new supervisor soon to take over. Suddenly a stranger, a lady who had been sitting unnoticed nearby, joined the conversation. "I heard you mention his name. He's the supervisor in my town (some distance away). I heard he was making a change." Whereupon she proceeded to relate some good things about him. My wife and her teacher-friend were relieved that the stranger had overheard only their positive remarks. "We were probably about to begin on the negative when she joined us."

REDUCING RUMORS

We'd all be better off spiritually if we could achieve rational control over our tongues. One cynic said the only way to do so would be by amputation. Since this solution is not likely to be widely practiced, here are some cautions that may help. Let's ask ourselves the following questions.

Is it true? The Bible commands, "Thou shalt not raise a false report" (Ex. 23:1).

Do not let yourself repeat a story until you have the facts. Don't hesitate to ask for evidence to support a rumor just passed on to you. Inquire and inquire diligently. If no substantiation is forthcoming, let the story stop right there. Often you may detect a bias or some hostility in the reporter. If so, the rumor is rendered less credible.

Accurate research often reveals that the incident never took place. Nero did not fiddle while Rome burned, for he was 30 miles away in his Antium villa at the time. Lady Godiva really existed, but she never rode naked atop a white horse.

A few years back a rumor circulated that the Social Security administration had accidentally issued an I.D. system with the ominous prophetical number 666 on it to several hundred Social Security recipients. A Christian financial adviser ran down every "hot" lead from someone who "knew" a person who had received one, but could not find one actual recipient.

More than once the words of Jesus were misconstrued. Witnesses testified that He had forbidden giving tribute to Caesar, and that He would destroy the temple and rebuild it in three days. Both allegations were wrong, for He had said, "Render tribute to Caesar," and the temple He referred to was His body, not the Jerusalem temple. Moreover, these witnesses were prejudiced.

Years ago I heard the story that the *Chicago Daily News* had its type all set up for the day of Christ's return with the startling news of thousands being caught up, leaving trains to run without engineers, cars without drivers, and homes missing loved ones. I used this striking bit of information more than once in my sermons. Then I decided to write Vaughn Shoemaker, then ace cartoonist for the *News*, as to the accuracy of the story. I received an emphatic denial. No print had been set up for such an event. His reply also mentioned this rumor had been going the rounds for years. He asked me to do whatever I could to squelch it.

Some large corporations combat rumor-mongers by denials publicly and frequently. They believe that making a rumor "news" changes its character, thus implying that anyone who passes it on is foolish and in error.

After Billy Graham's first visit to Moscow, all kinds of charges were leveled at the evangelist because of supposed statements during his public and private meetings. *Christianity Today* (June 18, 1982) ran an article, "Graham in Moscow: What Did He Really Say?" setting the record straight by showing how his words were taken out of context and wrongly used to betray his own deepest convictions. Also *The Christian Century* (June 23-30, 1982) published a story by Edward E. Plowman, "How the Press Got It Wrong in Moscow," in which he stated he tape-recorded all of Graham's public talks and most every one of his many press interviews with both Soviet and Western reporters. His conclusion, "Most of the criticism leveled against Graham in the West . . . rests on distorted and inaccurate reporting."

Someone said, "If you can't write it and sign it, don't say it." Good advice on the hearing end is, "When you hear an unsavory story about your neighbor, treat it as the cook does apples in making pies. First pare it, then quarter it; cut out the core, and use plenty of sugar with the rest."

Is it confidential? One of our daughters worked one summer at a large advertising agency in New York City. She was instructed never to discuss any detail or her work outside the office. "You never know who may overhear you in an elevator or restaurant."

The Bible says, "A talebearer revealeth secrets" (Prov. 11:13). Someone facetiously defined a secret as something you tell people one by one. Nevertheless, when a person tells you something in strict confidence, you should not divulge that secret. If you do, you break a confidence and qualify as a talebearer.

Betty was fond of Joan. Naturally, when Joan told her that she and her husband were having difficulty, she was deeply interested and so mentioned it to Margaret, her best friend. "Margaret's the kind you can trust. She doesn't go around gossiping," thought Betty. She said to Margaret, "You keep it a secret. Joan told me in strictest confidence!"

"Naturally," Margaret replied, "I won't tell anyone."

A week later Betty was walking down the street and saw Joan and her husband walking arm-in-arm, their difficulties apparently resolved. But a bigger surprise hit Betty when she was given the cold shoulder by the happy couple. She mumbled, "What did I do?"

Joan turned crimson, "I told you to keep it a secret about my husband and me. And you've blabbed it all over town. I didn't tell a soul beside you. It nearly broke up our marriage!"

Betty had told no one *except* Margaret, so she quickly phoned Margaret and learned she hadn't told anyone *except* her husband. "Oh, I tell him everything. All wives tell everything to their husbands."

Betty traced the story completely and discovered that no one had betrayed a confidence according to his or her standards, but had just mentioned it to *one* close associate who was "absolutely trustworthy." Margaret's husband mentioned it to his golf partner; the golf partner to his wife; the wife to her sister; the sister to her husband, who bowled with Joan's husband and who one night gently patted him on the back with, "It's sure tough when your marriage won't last." Betty learned her lesson the hard way, losing two friends and nearly ruining a marriage. Said the wise man, "He who repeats a matter alienates a friend" (Prov. 17:9, RSV). Says a proverb, "Three can keep a secret if two are dead."

Is it a cover-up for your own dirty linen or hang-ups? Perhaps we have a desire to be in the know. When we can inform others of some bit of little-known or classified information, it places us in the center of attention. We become the entertainer. We feel important when we can say, "Here's something practically no one else knows." Our center-stage role gives us a sense of power. Also, being in the know satisfies our curiosity.

The noted psychologist, Dr. Gordon Allport, explains it: "To be 'in the know' always exalts one's self-importance. While telling his tale, the gossiper finds himself socially dominant."

Uncertainty and anxiety help fuel rumors. One hypothesis says they are an effort to make sense out of the world and thus lessen apprehension. A rumor about some scary event makes a person shake his head and say, "It's a wicked jungle out there—not safe anywhere. And you can't trust anyone anymore." Even a rumor that scares a person as he tells it over and over may strangely reduce his anxiety and yield psychological solace.

Rumor-telling makes some people feel not only safe but superior. One person who struggled to break the gossip habit asked himself some questions: "Am I trying to lift my self-esteem by lowering my opinion of another?" "Think what he did. I'm not such a bad guy after all." "Could I be guilty of envying another's position, achievement, or honor, and wishing to tear him down a little?"

Analyzing our reasons for gossiping, as well as its content, may open our eyes to our weaknesses. Facing up to our short-comings will help us see we don't need a scapegoat on whom to project the things we don't like in ourselves. Seeking divine help may uncover and correct our low self-esteem, ill-will, or envy. Like Job, who said that he made a covenant with his eyes (Job 31:1), we need to make covenants with our mouths and ears if we hope to keep talebearing from blurring the image of Christ in us.

Is it necessary? A new church member was invited to join the Ladies Aid Society. Attending for the first time, she sat and listened to the conversation for a while, then left with these words, "This isn't the Ladies' Aid Society. It's the Ladies' Raid Society. You've spent every minute since I arrived in exposing the failures of people. Good-bye!"

A group of people do not help an absent party by unnecessarily repeating genuine faults. Just as taking a lovely flower and picking it to pieces, petal by petal, will dissipate its beauty, so will the pointless dissection of another's character fail to enhance his attractiveness.

Too many encouragements need to be given, too many commendations need to be passed on, too many vital matters need attention and discussion, to allow us to waste time and words on the foibles of others.

A 50-year-old lady, beset by both physical and family problems, told her doctor how miserable she felt. A compassionate person, he not only prescribed medicine, but listened sympathetically, as she fully unburdened herself. A week later a former neighbor remarked, "I hear you've been so depressed that you're in danger of losing your mind." When the lady recovered from her initial shock, she asked her former neighbor, "Where did you hear such a story?" She replied, "My daughter is a close friend of the nurse in the doctor's office." The lady became both humiliated and angry at this shocking breach of ethics by her doctor's nurse. How unnecessary to carry privileged information out of the office and pass it on as social gossip!

BE A GRAVEYARD FOR GOSSIP

Exposure to gossip is inevitable. How often we encounter, "They say." "Have you heard the latest scuttlebutt?" "I've a juicy tidbit to tell you." How should we respond? When you get bad TV, you switch channels. One man, fighting the gossip habit, lets his discomfort be known and changes the subject. For a while some friends cooled off a bit, but later respected his distaste of rumor. "For lack of wood the fire goes out; and where there is no whisperer, quarreling ceases" (Prov. 26:20, RSV).

If you must tell your story to someone, tell it to a wooden Indian, or to your child's doll, or to your dog or cat, or tell it to the birds, or to the wind. "A talebearer revealeth secrets: but he that is of a faithful spirit concealeth the matter" (Prov. 11:13). The concealer is a graveyard for gossip, weighing what he hears to make sure it is worthy of repeating. If the data is unworthy or doubtful, he promptly buries the tale. As a result, he probably will not hear too many tales, for a person who refuses to listen to gossip is soon left uninformed. A man had this motto on his dresser:

> What U say here,
> What U see here,
> Let it stay here,
> When U leave here.

A deacon heard a bit of gossip about an older preacher who had been a friend of his wife's family in earlier years. The preacher had been asked to leave not just one church, but two important pulpits, because of immorality, so the story ran. Though everything seemed to point to the likelihood of the gossip, the deacon had no way of investigating its accuracy. So he decided not to tell his wife, not wishing to destroy her respect for this old family friend who moved to the other side of the country and continued in Christian service till late life. More than once in the following years his wife crossed paths with the old preacher-friend and also received many letters from him, never suspecting the stigma of earlier decades.

A pastor's wife said that whenever she heard gossip, it was better to go, not to the phone, but to the throne.

We're never sorry for the things we do *not* say.

FOUR

EXAMINING YOUR EXCLAMATIONS

Norman Vincent Peale tells a story about Branch Rickey, head of the old Brooklyn Dodgers, who was attending a meeting to negotiate a contract for professional football at Ebbets Field. Suddenly Rickey threw down his pencil, pushed back his chair, and growled, "The deal's off."

Surprised, the other men asked why this abrupt break-off when all seemed going well on a deal involving big money for both sides. "Because," said Rickey, staring straight at one of the football representatives, "I don't like the way you've been talking about a friend of mine."

Bewildered, the football man responded, "But what friend? I haven't been talking about anyone, let alone a friend of yours."

"Oh, yes you have," countered Rickey. "You've mentioned Him in almost every sentence." Then he pointed out the man's repeated profane use of the name of Jesus Christ.

"I get you," said the other man quietly. "I won't do it again. You can count on it."

All too common is the careless introduction of God's name in conversation. Our ears tingle to hear that name flippantly juggled in every other sentence by thoughtless people.

A DEFINITION OF SWEARING

Swearing involves the irreverent use of God's name as a witness or party to some statement. Though often considered synonymous with profanity, blasphemy, and cursing, swearing is not identical with these. Profanity includes all irreverence of holy things, whereas swearing is but one type of sacrilege. Blasphemy means the intentional indignity offered God or holy things, but swearing is not always a direct, purposeful insult to God. Cursing or imprecation on another is but one branch of swearing, for while cursing foolishly implicates God's name with another's damnation, swearing embraces every manner of employment of God's name as a party to improper ends.

The telling of deliberate lies under oath. "Ye shall not swear by My name falsely," says the Lord (Lev. 19:12). Someone says, "So help me God, if this isn't true," and then proceeds to tell a deliberate falsehood. The reinforcement of a lie by the use of God's name is swearing.

Any witness who lies under oath in court is guilty not only of perjury but also of swearing, even if the answer just gives a false impression or contains a mental reservation. A man was asked by a judge if he had killed a certain person. "No," came the answer, and then under his breath he added, "No, not after I was arrested."

A man accused of slander was asked under oath if he had written a certain article. "I did not write it," was his reply, which in a measure was true, for he had not written it in person but had dictated it to his secretary.

In reality, both defendants were guilty of perjury and swearing. The name of God never should be linked with a lie! The dark depths of Peter's denial is understood more clearly when we remember that when he said he did not know Jesus, he said it with an oath.

Court oaths are not wrong, though some people doubt their propriety. It is easy to understand why some object to oaths. God's name is slurred over so as to render almost unintelligible the words of the person administering the oath. But if one really calls God to witness to the truth he is about to utter, he is not at fault.

Oaths were common in both the Old and New Testaments. Abraham made Eleazar, his steward, promise with an oath not to take a daughter of the Canaanites for Isaac's wife. "The Lord do so to me, and more also . . . (Ruth 1:17) were the words on Ruth's lips in pledging loyalty to her mother-in-law. More than once Paul called God to witness to some weighty utterance (2 Cor. 1:23; Phil. 1:8). Christ apparently was placed under oath when the high priest said, "I adjure Thee by the living God, that Thou tell us whether Thou be the Christ" (Matt. 26:63). An oath can be an act of worship and witness, for it recognizes God's existence, omniscience, and omnipresence; it admits His moral government over the world and the accountability of all men to Him as Judge. Of course, no atheist or skeptic has the right to take this oath.

The use of God's name in foolish oaths. In the days of Christ the practice of swearing to trifles had become well established. People of today would not invoke God's name on unimportant matters, such as crossing a street or sitting in a chair. Yet the people of Christ's day would call God to witness to such insignificant things.

To their credit, however—due to their literal observance of the Third Commandment, "Thou shalt not take the name of the Lord thy God in vain"—they seldom pronounced God's name but substituted other words such as "the Most High," "the King of heaven," "heaven," "Jerusalem." That is why Jesus ordered, "Swear not at all: neither by heaven, for it is God's throne; nor by the earth, for it is His footstool; neither by Jerusalem, for it is the city of the great King. Neither shalt thou swear by thy head, because thou canst not make one hair white or black. But let your communication be, Yea, yea; Nay, nay; for whatsoever is more than these cometh of evil" (Matt. 5:34-37).

Foolish oaths likewise come under the category of swearing, such as King Saul's swearing on the day of battle a curse on any man eating food before evening (1 Sam. 14:24). His own son Jonathan, who didn't hear the curse pronounced, ate. But his life was saved by the people. Centuries later 40 men promised with an oath not to eat or drink until they killed Paul (Acts 23:21). This rash and evil oath undoubtedly was not kept.

The use of God's name in moments of anger. How often we hear someone in a moment of temper exclaim, "God damn you." This is either asking God to do something unworthy of Himself or unthinkingly introducing God's name as a vent for anger, both of which are irreverent uses.

The use of God's name as conversation fillers. Sometimes, when unnecessary words are removed from conversation, little of importance remains. A policeman was asked by the judge what the prisoner had said when arrested. "Leaving out the bad language, Judge?" asked the policeman.

"Yes," replied the judge.

"Not a word."

Many words that we use unwittingly to fill up conversation are swearwords. A casual reading of even the most widely acclaimed prose and poetry reveals how prone the human tongue is to drag God into the most trivial of affairs. We hear people exclaim in moments of surprise, "My God!" "Good God!" "O Lord!" They demote God's name to an exclamation mark! Or when

someone sneezes, another person reacts with, "God bless you!"
Or when one of the family retires to bed, others say, "God bless
you!" If the heart desires God's blessing as the mouth frames the
word, this is good and proper, but if not, God's name is used
thoughtlessly.

The reply to a question may be, "Only God Almighty
knows!" There may be times when the reference is really to
divine omniscience, but often it's just a flippant remark. Similarly, when our word is doubted, we may lightly preface our
protest, "Honest to God."

Since God's attributes often explain the divine name, the
thoughtless use of any quality describing God may be considered
irreverent. "Holy Joe!" "Good gracious!" "Merciful me!"
each contain an attribute that belongs to Deity alone. Thus to
speak superficially of any divine attribute is to speak lightly of
God's name.

Many slang expressions are nothing but substitutions and
variations of powerful swearwords. For centuries Englishmen
have been famed for the forthrightness and frequency of their
oaths. "By the splendor of God" was William the Conqueror's
favorite oath. Henry II swore by God's eyes, another by God's
tooth. So impressive were some medieval swearers that their
children inherited names that memorialized their profane art.
Surnames in English history included "Godbode," "God-me-
fetch," "Godsowl." The favorite name the French gave the
Englishman in their plays was "John Goddano." Servants in
medieval England could swear profusely but never with the
variety and delicacy of their masters. A gentleman seldom
opened his mouth without calling on his Creator to curse, sink,
confound, or blast someone.

Then, as time went on, favorite oaths were shortened and
stereotyped so that today these swearwords are used in their
abbreviated forms by people who do not realize the oaths they

are employing. Professors of languages inform us that "by God's wounds" became "zounds"; "God's blood" became "by gad"; "by God" became "by gum." For "Jesus" the following forms developed: "gee whiz," "jeeze," "Jerusalem," "gee," and "gee whillikins." Instead of "Christ," there came "cripes," "jiminy Christmas," "jeepers creepers," and "for crying out loud." "Lord" gave way to "lawdy" and "law sakes."

It has been suggested that "gee" is merely the first letter of "God" and the first syllable of "Jesus"—a coward's way of swearing. "Gosh" is "God" with the final letter shaded into a slur as though ashamed to utter it. "Godamighty" is slurred "God Almighty," while "doggone it" and "darn it" are but plays on "God damn it."

Perhaps you protest, "I say these words but don't mean anything by them." That is just the point. That is just what the third commandment forbids: "Thou shalt not take the name of the Lord without meaning something by it."

THE FOOLISHNESS OF SWEARING

In Chaucer's "Canterbury Tales" as the pilgrims journeyed toward Canterbury, they swore by Christ, His body, and His wounds until the "for God's bones and by God's dignity" drove the sincere parson to protest, "What aileth the man so sinfully to swear?" He was only asking a question that baffles explanation: "Why do men swear?"

How men fall into the habit is easily explained. The mind ruffled by excitement seeks a safety valve. It seizes on expressions which the person has heard others utter in moments of emotional strain. After giving vent to one's feelings a few times with swearwords, it becomes easy. Then it is indulged in as luxury when the mind is undisturbed and unruffled.

The pointlessness of swearing. If there were some profit in swearing, we might understand why people swear. "Ten Reasons Why I Swear" is the humorous title of a tract written by Alex Dunlap, which shows the foolishness of the habit.

1. It pleases mother so much.
2. It is a fine mark of manliness.
3. It proves I have self-control.
4. It indicates how clearly my mind operates.
5. It makes my conversation so pleasing to everybody.
6. It leaves no doubt in anyone's mind as to my good breeding.
7. It impresses people that I have more than an ordinary education.
8. It is an unmistakable sign of culture and refinement.
9. It makes me a very desirable personality among women and children and respectable society.
10. It is my way of honoring God, who said, "Thou shalt not take the name of the Lord thy God in vain."

Most bewildering of all is the practice of taking the name of Christ in vain. When we consider that He came from heaven to shed His blood for us, we wonder how anyone could use that name in profanity. We would never speak disparagingly of our mothers. Why speak flippantly of Christ, whose love far exceeds that of the fondest mother?

Swearing is neither smart, sensible, nor worthwhile. A traveling salesman was once asked, "Are you paid anything for swearing?"

"No," he replied.

"Well," came the answer, "you certainly work cheap. You lay aside your character as a gentleman, inflict pain on your friends, break a commandment, lose your own soul, and all for nothing!"

The poison of swearing. Years ago in England a nobleman visited the Wedgwood Factory, famous for pottery, and was shown around by a lad of 15. Mr. Wedgwood followed a few steps behind. During the tour the English peer, a recklessly irreverent man, though a brilliant conversationalist, shocked and then captivated the lad, who began to laugh heartily at his profanity. When the tour was over, Mr. Wedgwood sat in his office with the nobleman. Holding up a beautiful vase before the peer who was about to receive it, Mr. Wedgwood deliberately dropped it on the floor, shattering it in countless pieces. Angrily the peer demanded, "Why did you do that?"

Came the reply, "There are other things more precious than this piece of pottery. Sir, I can make you another vase as beautiful as this, but you cannot give back that boy his former simple faith and reverence which you have destroyed with your irreverent talk!"

When children, too young to know the meaning of the words they utter, hurl blasphemous oaths at each other in their play, adults should not be shocked, for they are only hearing their own language come home. When it is the practice in a home to take God's name in vain and curse in terms of gigantic hatred on the least provocation, children will imitate every inflection and tone.

Not only does swearing poison the character of others but it has a deadening effect on the guilty party. The one who habitually speaks lightly of God's name will not easily run to that One in the hour of need. "The name of the Lord is a strong tower: the righteous runneth into it, and is safe" (Prov. 18:10). The swearer finds it embarrassing and difficult to implore God's mercy and aid.

The punishability of swearing. "Oh, it's just a bad habit," does not excuse swearing. A criminal arraigned before a judge for stealing could never hope to gain acquittal by pleading that stealing was just a habit with him.

The Decalogue is most specific. Its third commandment says, "Thou shalt not take the name of the Lord thy God in vain; for the Lord will not hold him guiltless that taketh His name in vain" (Ex. 20:7). Scripture gives warning of the serious nature of this offense in the story of a son of an Israelitish woman and an Egyptian father. The lad swore. Moses ordered him stoned to death outside the camp (Lev. 24:23).

Said the poet Cowper:

> It chills my blood to hear the blest Supreme
> Rudely appealed to on each trifling theme!
> Maintain your rank; vulgarity despise;
> To swear is neither brave, polite, nor wise.
> You would not swear upon the bed of death;
> Reflect! Your Maker now could stop your breath!

HOW TO OVERCOME SWEARING

Many modern theorists of swearing regard foul language as a valuable safety valve that helps society function without too much frustration. Used judiciously, it is claimed, swearwords can salvage self-esteem and rescue one's ego from ruin. In addition, many of today's younger set deem it fashionable to swear.

But the Word of God is clearly against all unsavory speech, including swearwords.

Some brief suggestions to help defeat the habit of swearing are in order.

A need for forgiveness. A sergeant in charge of a mess hall during World War II was concerned over the swearing there, for many of the workers at the time were women. So he devised a plan. He took a quart fruit jar, sealed it up, cut a slot in the lid, and labeled it, "Swear can—5 cents for each profane word."

Five cents will not atone for our cursing. Swearing is so serious that it took the death of Christ to merit forgiveness. If there had been only one sin in the world and that sin was swearing and it had been committed just once, Jesus Christ still would have died to pay for it.

The depth of the source. Mothers sometimes warn their children, "If you don't stop your foul language, I'll wash your mouth with soap!" Washing one's mouth with soap will not get rid of the cause of swearing. The root of the trouble lies deeper— in the heart. It takes the regenerating power of Christ to transform the moral base and give new motivation. As the wise man said, "Keep thy heart with all diligence; for out of it are the issues of life" (Prov. 4:23). We first need the new birth by receiving Christ as our Saviour so that the wellspring of our speech may be given a divine restraint.

Wariness of substitution. Examine your verbal ejaculations in moments of surprise. Ask someone to point out the expressions you use most in conversation which in reality are just variations of swearwords. Fight by God's grace to rid yourself of their usage, even more earnestly than you would strive to overcome some grammatical mistake of which you were constantly guilty. The transformation of any sacreligious speech patterns is part of our ongoing sanctification.

Control of anger. Many people vent their anger in unbridled expressions, including cursing and swearing. Some people have learned to control their anger to some degree by using less vehement forms of speech. A mother, president of her local PTA, was taken aback when her 11-year-old son began to swear. Realizing he was going through some changes, she allowed it to go on for a while, then finally suggested that with his interest in vocabulary perhaps he and his friends might find other ways to rake one another over the coals without using foul words. She reported how they became sophisticated, using a lot of colorful language from Shakespeare. But raking others over the coals, even though with high-class words, betrays a deficiency in self-control.

A preacher driving along a narrow highway accidentally crowded a truck off into the ditch. Emerging from his cab, the truck driver swore profusely at the preacher, who responded, "I suppose you are aware that I am a preacher and unable to use such language, but I certainly hope that when you get home your mother-in-law runs out from under your porch and bites you." Though displaying amusing ingenuity and patience, the preacher's reply was not a complete victory over improper speech.

Some psychologists would say that if in fixing a cabinet you hit your thumb with the hammer, instead of hammering the cabinet to pieces, it's better to let out some swearwords and thus relieve the tension and restore some physical calm to the body. But is there not another choice? Cannot a victim vent his exasperation by exclaiming, "Ouch!" as many times as he wishes, perhaps adding a few "It hurts!" Then he could say, "I must be more careful. I must not let the hammer slip again." Instead of throwing a tantrum we should acknowledge our pain, admit our mistake, and affirm determination to bring about a positive change. Sounds idealistic, but let's not forget that the last virtue in the list of the fruit of the Spirit is self-control, which means literally, "inner strength" (Gal. 5:23). Paul wrote, "Be ye angry, and sin not" (Eph. 4:26).

Cultivation of a sense of reverence. The father of Woodrow Wilson, a distinguished Presbyterian minister, sat with a group of men who were having a heated discussion when suddenly one of the men uttered an oath. Then, noticing Dr. Wilson, apologized, "Sir, I forgot that you were present." The preacher replied, "It's not to me that you owe your apology, but to God."

Think of God—the only true God, omnipotent, omnipresent, omniscient, unchangeable, independent, holy, righteous, loving.

Think of what God has done—His watchcare, providence, and above all His gift of Christ. Think how Christ suffered on our behalf. If you do this, respect and awe for His divine name will grow until it will be impossible to use it frivolously.

Also, we need to cultivate a sense of God's presence. If we were in the presence of some earthly potentate, we would not speak lightly of his name. If we recall that we are always in God's presence, we shall be careful in our use of His name. It is said that Sir Isaac Newton never mentioned God in conversation without a visible pause, and if his head was covered at the time, he customarily raised his hat.

One man trying to get victory over his long habit of ejaculating, "O God!" followed this rule. Every time he said, "O God," he didn't stop there, but made it into a prayer that started, "O God—how great Thou art!" Then adoringly, worshipfully, he repeated, "For how really great Thou art, O God!"

How urgent to keep praying, "Hallowed be Thy name," until that day when every knee shall bow and every tongue shall confess the name which is above every other name.

FIVE

FORKED LIGHTNING

bitter message, discovered on a marble gravestone slab in Milford, New Hampshire, charged a church with murdering one of its lady members by gossip and false accusations. After her name were these words: "Murdered by the Baptist Ministry and churches, as follows, Sept. 28, 1838. Age 33, she was accused of lying in Church Meeting by the pastor and a Deacon [their names are given], was condemned by the church unheard. She was reduced to poverty." At this point the gravestone stated that the Milford Baptist Church closed the matter to all discussion, then continued, "The intentional and malicious destruction of her character and happiness, as above described, destroyed her life. Her last words upon the subject were, 'Tell the truth and this iniquity will come out' " (Wallis, *Stories on Stone*, Oxford, 1954).

No sin of speech has as many warnings as slander. The psalmist David says the "tongue plots destruction; it is like a sharpened razor" (52:2, NIV). The proverbist says, "The words of the wicked lie in wait for blood" (Prov. 12:6, NIV). Jezebel caused Naboth's death through a false charge. The last word of Romans 1:29 is "whisperers" and the first word of Romans 1:30 is "backbiters." In the *Revised Standard Version* these words are "gossips" and "slanderers." James describes the tongue as "a fire, a world of iniquity," warning, "Speak not evil one of another, brethren (James 3:6; 4:11).

The Chairman of United Technologies ran a large ad about slander in several national publications. He titled it, "The Snake that Poisons Everybody." Part of the copy read, "It topples governments, wrecks marriages, ruins careers, bursts reputations, causes heartaches, nightmares, indigestion, spawns suspicions, generates grief, dispatches innocent people to cry in their pillows. It makes headlines and heartaches."

SLANDER MORE THAN RUMOR AND GOSSIP

Slander is an advance upon rumor and gossip. Whereas a babbler speaks thoughtlessly of others, a slanderer speaks harmfully of others. Rumor and gossip do not necessarily impugn another's reputation, but slander is always vicious and malicious, vilifying a good name by deliberate misrepresentation, whispered insinuation, or subtle innuendo. Shakespeare wrote,

> Who steals my purse steals trash. . . .
> But he that filches from me my good name
> Robs me of that which not enriches him,
> And makes me poor indeed.

Dr. Ralph L. Rosnow, a communications theorist at Temple University in his book, *Rumor and Gossip* (1976), mentions three broad categories of rumors: pipe dreams, bogies, and wedge-drivers. A report that my stock is going to rise sharply is an example of a pipe dream or wish-rumor. A story of terror at the mall is a bogie type. The wedge-driving rumor causes division among people and groups, and is slanderous. Analysis of more than 1,000 rumors revealed that more than 66 percent were wedge-drivers, thus injuring people.

Evangelicals were victimized by bigotry more than any other group during the 1984 political campaigns, according to Dr. Michael Novak, Roman Catholic sociologist. Writing in the Anti-Defamation League Bulletin of B'nai B'rith, he said that "code words without the existence of evidence and a string of associations are techniques used to engender fear and elicit hatred and contempt" (From *Evangelical Newsletter*, vol. 11, no. 24, Dec. 21, 1984, Philadelphia, PA).

AGAINST INSTITUTIONS

Often slander is directed against institutions. Since 1980 Proctor & Gamble has been the victim of nasty rumors which connect the company with devil worship. One flier, urging a boycott of the the company's products, erroneously said the company executives admitted the connection publicly on either the Phil Donahue or the Merv Griffin program.

At the heart of the rumor is the company's trademark, a crescent-shaped man in the moon and 13 stars. A company representative states that the moon-and-stars symbol represents only P&G, and has no other associations. The man-in-the-moon profile was all the rage back in 1882 when P&G patented its trademark. The 13 stars merely signify the 13 original stars in our flag, and evolved from a single-star insignia P&G used to identify crates of Star Candles shipped down the Ohio River as early as 1851.

The company thought it had banished the rumor in 1982 after the flood of inquiries on its toll-free telephone lines peaked at

15,000 in one month. At that time the company turned tough, secured supporting testimonials from Jerry Falwell and Billy Graham because the rumor had received its first big boost from Protestant fundamentalists. P&G also filed 6 lawsuits against some who had spread the rumor, claiming that all but one of the defendants sold products of competing companies. But in 1984 the rumors cropped up anew. Noting that over 100,000 consumers had called or written about the rumors, P&G decided in 1985 to drop the controversial trademark from its products.

Did you know that in the 1930s business services specialized in spreading rumors in our country, created mainly by professional rumor-mongers to capture sales from one manufacturer to another? One rumor claimed that a leper was working in a certain cigarette factory. Another said a certain company had made a large contribution to help Hitler.

Though such business services may now be nonexistent, harmful rumors keep cropping up here and there. A few years ago a rumor spread through the Greater New York area that Bubble Yum, the hottest thing to have hit the chewing gum industry since sugarless gum, had spider eggs in it. The rumor slowed down the sales of Bubble Yum. Drugstores that sold 60 or 70 packs a day fell to one or two.

McDonalds suffered a 20 percent drop in sales in the southwest in 1978 when a baseless rumor spread that worms had been added to their hamburgers. It then began a media campaign that emphasized the use of "100 percent pure beef." Also, the well-known Entenmann's bakery had to deny a widely circulated rumor that it was owned by "the Moonies."

AGAINST PERSONS
Though slander has often been aimed at institutions, it has probably done its most damage against individuals. Madam

Curie, the radium genius, bravely continued her work after the untimely death of her husband. Suffering severe loneliness, for she had been deeply in love with her husband, she was consoled by a handful of close friends who did their best to heal the gaping wound. Tragically, terrible talkers in Paris struck out against Madam Curie, all because, naturally, a couple of men had been close associates in her laboratories. The whispers grew to widely publicized slurs and gross untruths. The lies cut deeply until this exhausted, brokenhearted widow actually contemplated suicide. She never did fully recover from the assault of those false accusing voices.

A column in the *Washington Post* once suggested that President Carter had placed electronic devices in Blair House, across from the White House, to spy on Ronald Reagan. Under threat of a libel suit the *Post* finally retracted the item and apologized to Mr. Carter.

Jerry Falwell recently won a suit he brought against publisher Larry Flynt for libelous remarks. But many untold thousands are never awarded anything despite the heavy damages suffered from the slanderous remarks of others.

In Chapter 4 we suggested several questions to ask ourselves before passing on any rumor or gossip. Is it true? Is it confidential? Is it a cover-up for our dirty linen or hang-ups? Is it necessary? We now add a final test. Is it *kind?*

POWER OF INNUENDO

In *Psychology Today* (February 1982) an article titled, "Would This Magazine Print Innuendo?" reported on studies which indicated that people tend to put almost as much stock in innuendo as they do in fact. In one experiment 48 college undergraduates were asked their reactions to fictitious newspaper headlines purportedly appearing two weeks before an election. One headline hinted that a certain candidate might have had links with the Mafia; the other headline made a direct charge. The students tended to believe the innuendo as much as those headlines with direct accusations.

In another study half the students were told the headlines had appeared in a reliable publication, while the other half were told the captions had appeared in a scandal sheet. Both groups accepted the headlines as credible, regardless of the source. How true this also is in Christian circles! We hear scandal about a Christian leader. The rumor is proven untrue and recanted by the accuser. Yet we tend to attach that scandal to that leader's name whenever his name is mentioned.

IRRETRIEVABILITY OF SCANDALOUS WORDS

It would not be so bad if our talebearing stopped with the person into whose ears we whispered. But after our words leave our lips, it is absolutely impossible to recall them. They may go the rounds from person to person and country to country, finally to be recalled in that day when men shall give an account for every idle word.

One day a lady went to her pastor to make a confession. She admitted she was a slanderer and asked him to assign her some penance.

The pastor asked, "Do you frequently fall into this fault?"

"Yes," she replied, "very often."

Then he prescribed, "Go to the nearest market and purchase a chicken just killed but still covered with feathers. Walk through the streets of town, plucking the bird as you go. Then return to me."

The lady did as she was told and in a short while returned to make her report. The pastor then said, "You have been very faithful to the first part of my orders; now do the second part and you will be cured. Retrace your steps, passing through all the places you have traversed, and gather up one by one all the feathers you have scattered."

"But, Pastor," she replied, "I cast the feathers carelessly on each side. The wind has blown them in every direction. How can I recover them?"

"Well, my child," answered the old pastor, "so it is with your words of slander. Like the feathers which the wind scattered, they have been wafted in many directions. Call them back now, if you can."

When an unkind story was going the rounds in a midwest town, a young man exclaimed in a cafe, "I'd like to see that story traced back." A club was organized, incorporating a noble set of rules, and naming itself, "Trace It Back Club." Whenever a person opened his mouth to incriminate another, a member would speak up with, "I appoint a committee to trace back that story." For a while the club showed promise, but it soon went the way of all flesh.

> Boys flying kites haul in their white-winged birds,
> But you can't do that when you're flying words.

HANDLING SLANDERERS

In *The Idylls of the King*, Arthur told Guinevere that he had instructed his Knights of the Round Table "to speak no slander; no, nor listen to it." Easier said than done.

Carl Holliday in his book, *Woman's Life in Colonial Days* (p. 289ff), tells how in Virginia in the 17th century a wife convicted of slander was carried to the dunking stool and dunked unless her husband consented to pay the fine imposed for the offense. In that same period a woman residing in Northampton, Massachusetts was punished for defamation by a sentence to stand at the door of her parish church during the singing of the psalm, with a gag in her mouth. Another lady was ordered to go to the house of the woman she had slandered and beg her forgiveness.

One lady had an effective stopper for scandal. Whenever told anything derogatory of another, her immediate reply was, "Come, we will go and ask that person if it is true." The effect was often comically painful. The talebearer sometimes begged that the statement be stricken from the record, or quickly quali-fied its wording, or stammered out a partial retraction. But the lady was persistent. Often she took the scandal-speaker to the scandalized to compare accounts. The likelihood of that person venturing a second time to repeat a story to her was virtually nil. Also, that person likely thereafter gave careful thought before spilling scandal to anyone. As Paul wrote, "Do not entertain an accusation against an elder unless it is brought by two or three witnesses" (1 Tim. 5:19, NIV).

TRAGIC POTENTIAL OF SLANDER

The following incident which took place a few years back portrays the terrible defamatory potential of carelessly communi-cated charges. Names have been changed.

Bill Jackson hurried through his chores to go to the Scout meeting, arriving just in time to answer the roll call. Bill and his mother managed a small farm and eked out a living by selling milk to a few of the townsfolk. Bill's father, a heavy drinker, paid little attention to matters at home. The Scout meeting closed early since the assistant scoutmaster was in charge. Just as the boys were about to leave, someone exclaimed, "Say, do you see what I see?"

"What?" questioned the others in chorus.

"Look there! Someone's brought a bottle of beer to the Scout meeting!"

In the excitement of discovery someone said, "It's easy to tell where that came from. Bill's dad is the only father who's a drinker. It isn't hard to know who brought the bottle!"

Some agreed. Others tried to defend Bill, who, stung by the accusation, said, "I couldn't have brought the bottle because I came late tonight. And furthermore, you know how I hate the stuff because of what it's done to my father. I'm sorry you don't trust me." Deeply hurt, he left with a heavy heart.

Tom Brown, who made the accusation, dared the boys to take a sip of the bottle, and they tasted its contents. Tom finished the bottle. When he arrived home, his mother, startled at the odor of his breath, asked, "Tom, when did they start having liquor at Scout meetings?"

"Tonight, Mother. Bill Jackson brought it. You know his father is a drunkard and he can get it easy. He passed the bottle around and I finished it."

"Well, the very idea! I'm going to make it hard for Bill Jackson!" Hurrying to the phone, she called the pastor. "Pastor, I demand you do something about that Bill Jackson being a Scout!"

"Why, he's a good Scout!" answered the pastor.

"No, he isn't," interrupted Mrs. Brown. "Do you know what happened tonight at the Scout meeting? He brought several bottles of liquor and made the boys drink it. Why weren't you there?"

"I had a cold, and the assistant Scout leader is very capable."

"Well, see what happened tonight!" retorted the irate Mrs. Brown.

"I'm very sorry," said the pastor. "I'll take care of it."

Then Mrs. Brown called the town mayor and told him the boys had used half a dozen bottles of liquor. The mayor promised to look into it.

The next day a special assembly was called at school. First the mayor spoke, then the pastor. They told how the night before the Boy Scouts had used half a case of liquor, and they knew who had brought it. They named Bill Jackson and advised his schoolmates to shun him. Bill hurried home and told his mother. After chores he said, "Mother, I'm going to have a talk with the pastor and the mayor. They should know I'm not to blame."

The mayor refused to believe Bill. Sternly he said, "The blame is on you until you tell who did it. Before long we may send you to the state training school." Deeply grieved, Bill headed for his pastor, sure that he would receive help there. But the man who should have known better was most unfriendly. "Bill, confirmation time is approaching. I know you've looked forward to it for a long time, but unless you confess who brought the liquor to Scout meeting, I cannot confirm you!"

"O Pastor, you wouldn't do that!"

"All I can say is, if you decide to confess before confirmation Sunday, come to me and I'll let you be in the class. Think it over."

Utterly despondent, Bill went home and told his mother, who likewise grieved at her son's mistreatment. Next morning when Bill went out early to sell his milk, scarcely a person would buy from him. Mrs. Brown's tongue had been busy. School was a nightmare. His appetite dwindled. But he could sleep at night, for his conscience was clear.

Not so with Tom. At night he could not sleep, especially when he knew confirmation would be denied Bill. So he decided to straighten matters up somewhat. He told his mother that it was only one bottle of liquor that had been found at Scout meeting and that Bill had not asked the others to drink. Mrs. Brown immediately phoned the mayor and the pastor. However, they both insisted that unless Bill confessed or told who brought the bottle, he would have to go to the state training school and would not be confirmed. It was the Monday before confirmation. The week went by. Saturday came. Bill hurried with the chores. "Mother, I want one more talk with the pastor."

Bill went to the parsonage but was informed that the pastor was out. Again in the afternoon he tried and received the same answer. "Mother," he asked, "do you suppose it would do any good to try again?"

"Son, you've come home from each visit feeling worse. Perhaps even if you saw him you would feel terrible."

"You're right, Mother! You mentioned you wanted to make a visit tonight. You go out and I'll stay home."

So Bill's mother went. When she came home, she couldn't find him. She called but there was no answer. She went out to the barn, and there a terrible sight met her eyes. Bill's body hung from a rafter, a rope around his neck. When the doctor arrived and learned all the poor boy had suffered in recent weeks, he commented, "This boy didn't die by hanging. He died of a broken heart."

His father, completely sobered, sat beside his wife through the long hours of the night sobbing. "Oh, my boy, killed because of liquor you refused to touch!"

When the neighbors heard, they came, but their sympathy was too late. The pastor did not come till after the confirmation service, but he wept profusely because of his treatment of the boy. Bill's father asked the pastor to take the funeral service.

Tom, terrified at the news of Bill's death, confessed to his mother that Bill had not brought the bottle at all. Later the school janitor took his life, drawing suspicion that he was responsible for the bottle's presence. Mrs. Brown dropped her head in shame that she had blamed Bill falsely, arousing the town against him.

The night before the funeral the pastor paced the floor, weeping and praying. The hour for the funeral came. The choir that had sung for confirmation sang for Bill. The pastor preached a sermon, then made a confession. "I have failed Bill. He tried to contact me Saturday several times, but I was too busy getting ready for the confirmation service to talk with him. His heart was broken at the treatment he received, and I've asked the Lord to forgive me. We have all failed him. As you pass by Bill today, you will see in his hand the confirmation certificate he so badly wanted. He deserved it, so we are giving it to him, though too late. As you pass by, think of your failings and ask Christ to forgive you your sins; resolve never to fail one of God's children."

While the organ played, they passed by—the Scouts who had failed a fellow member when he needed them; the mayor who had failed to believe a truthful boy; the teachers and students who had snubbed him; the women who had refused to buy milk from him; Tom, who had deliberately lied; and Mrs. Brown, whose tongue had been one of the main causes of his mistreatment (used by permission of Union Gospel Press).

No one this side of judgment day can measure the havoc caused by a slandering tongue. "A tongue three inches long can kill a man six feet tall." Said Ben Johnson, "Slander cuts men's throats with whisperings." He who slanders does the devil's work, for one of Satan's major names is "accuser of the brethren." In fact, devil means slander or slanderous. Dr. A.B. Simpson, founder of the Christian and Missionary Alliance, said, "I would rather play with forked lightning or take in my hands living wires, with their fiery currents, than speak a reckless word against any servant of Christ, or idly repeat the slanderous darts which thousands of Christians are hurling on others."

Rather, Christian love thinks no evil but rejoices in the truth, bearing, believing, and hoping all things (1 Cor. 13:5-7). Paul commands, "Let no evil talk come out of your mouths, but only such as is good for edifying, as fits the occasion, that it may impart grace to those who hear" (Eph. 4:29, RSV).

SIX

DO YOU NEEDLE PEOPLE?

A fable tells of a careless old hen in a farmer's barnyard. Accidentally she stepped on a duck's foot. It did not hurt the duck, but the duck got peeved and said, "I'll pay you for that!" So the duck flew at the old hen; but as he did so, his wings struck an old goose that was standing near.

The old goose became angry and, thinking it was done on purpose, said to the duck, "I'll pay you for that!" And with that he flew at the duck. As he did so, his foot tore the fur of a cat that was taking a sun bath.

"I'll pay you for that!" hissed the cat, as she started for the goose. But as she jumped, her foot struck a ram.

"I'll pay you for that!" bleated the ram, and he made a dash for the cat. But just then a dog ran that way, and the ram ran over the dog.

"I'll pay you for that!" barked the dog, and ran pell-mell after the ram. He ran so fast that he could not avoid the cow that stood by the gate and ran smack against her.

"I'll pay you for that!" bellowed the cow, and started after the dog. But the dog ran behind a horse, and the cow, in her haste, scratched the horse with her horns.

"I'll pay you for that!" neighed the horse, and rushed at the cow.

What a tumult there was! The duck chased the hen; the goose, the duck; the cat, the goose; the ram, the cat; the dog, the ram; the cow, the dog; and the horse, the cow. And all this took place because the hen had accidentally stepped on the duck's toes.

Startled by the commotion, the farmer ran out and soon had the scrappers locked up in their respective domiciles, their good times over for the day, all because they would not overlook a little unintentional hurt.

Contention is sometimes avoidable, but many times contention can be avoided by the circumspect use of the tongue. When conviction and principles are at stake, then one must contend for the right. We are urged to contend for the faith. The priests did right when they contended against King Uzziah for his intrusion into the priest's office to burn incense in the temple (2 Chron. 26:16-21). John the Baptist's contentious words were justified when he told Herod that it was not lawful for him to take his brother's wife. We do not consider a policeman contentious when he charges a criminal with breaking the law. It is the lawbreaker who has disturbed the peace. When there is wrong, the right needs to be urged, even if some contention results.

But though it is sometimes necessary and healthy to contend, too often we are contentious in our contention.

WHAT ARE CONTENTIOUS WORDS?

A wasp buzzes momentarily around your head as you amble down the street. If you do not bother it, the chances are that it will not bother you. But try to swat it, and you may stir up the wasp to fly at you and sting you.

In some situations the utterance of certain remarks will stir up a hornets' nest. When you speak words that rub against the grain, or wave a red flag in front of someone present, you're inviting an argument. Comments that stir up or fuel a fuss are "fightin' words." An uncivil answer to a civil question may ignite a spark. A motion at a business meeting to spite a minority group may lead to combat. A contemptuous question, such as wealthy Nabal's retort to fugitive David, "Who is David? And who is the son of Jesse?" the equivalent of, "Who do you think you are?" invites retaliation.

Nagging is a form of criticism which Proverbs likens to a constant dripping on a rainy day (Prov. 27:15). A wife who repeatedly warns her husband to be home on time for dinner, or the husband who reminds his wife a dozen times to be sure and do the ironing may be hastening their marital grave by such little "digs."

Someone listed clichés which, to keep friends and home happy, should never be uttered: "I wouldn't let him get away with that"; "She's just jealous, that's all"; "He thinks he's somebody, but I remember when. . . "; "Don't be mad if I tell you this, but. . . "; "I think you should know what she said about you"; "After all, I have my pride."

In an editorial in *Christianity Today* (Oct. 19, 1984) titled " 'Tis the Season for Invective," V. Gilbert Beers and Harold Smith point out that during the presidential campaigns the American electorate heard Walter Mondale call Gary Hart a "cold-hearted wretch," and Jesse Jackson assailed as an "anti-Semite," and Geraldine Ferraro openly question President Reagan's Christianity by alluding to his "meanness to poor people and his penchant for nuclear war." Mondale was labeled by the Republicans as a "born loser" suffering from a "wimp factor."

The editorial also pointed out some much stronger language used in past campaigns. In his unsuccessful bid for president in 1796, Thomas Jefferson was described by the opposition party as an anarchist, demagogue, atheist, trickster, and coward, while his followers were depicted as "cutthroats who walk in rags and sleep amidst filth and vermin." Horace Greeley, soundly beaten by Civil War hero Ulysses S. Grant in the 1872 election, complained, "I have been assailed so bitterly that I hardly knew if I was running for the presidency or the penitentiary."

Sadly, Christians today often stoop to mudslinging, ugly rhetoric, and the hurling of thunderbolts at each other. In the last few years Christian leaders have been known to call their fellow-Christians "spineless," "a lot of jellyfish," and some have even questioned the sanity of other believers.

DANGERS OF THE CONTENTIOUS TONGUE

Anger. The most frequent danger of the contentious tongue is its potential for anger, both on the part of the person saying pugnacious things and the person listening. Contentiousness leads to hot retorts, angry remarks, lost tempers, and sometimes actual bodily conflicts. Anger is potential murder. That is why Jesus warned, "Whosoever is angry with his brother without a cause shall be in danger of the judgment" (Matt. 5:22).

Though there is such a thing as righteous indignation, most folks must confess that their wrath usually springs not from love of righteous principles but from hurt feelings and injured pride. Losing one's temper wounds others and rebounds on oneself. "A harsh word stirs up anger" (Prov. 15:1, NIV). A good percentage of murders result from family disputes.

When I have lost my temper I have lost my reason too,
I'm never proud of anything which angrily I do

When I have talked in anger and my cheeks were flaming red,
I have always uttered something which I wish I hadn't said.
In anger I have never done a kindly deed or wise,
But many things for which I felt I should apologize.
In looking back across my life, and all I've lost or made,
I can't recall a single time when fury ever paid.
So I struggle to be patient, for I've reached a wiser age;
I do not want to do a thing or speak a word in rage.
I have learned by sad experience that when my temper flies
I never do a worthy thing, a decent deed or wise.

—Author unknown

Name-calling. As the Yankees took the field for the opening game of the 1932 World Series against the Chicago Cubs, all the Yankees were blazing with resentment, Babe Ruth most of all. For a former teammate, recently traded to the Cubs, had been voted only a quarter share of the World Series prize money. So Ruth boomed to his former teammate, "Who are those cheapskates with you?" The silent Cubs squirmed uncomfortably. "Nickel-nursers!" taunted Ruth. "Misers!" The rest was unprintable.

These words of contention caused the Cubs to strike back angrily with a verbal assault of their own, Babe Ruth being the principal target. By the third game the insults were blistering enough to curl a fellow's hair. In addition, the crowd had taken up the chant and rode Babe Ruth mercilessly. Ruth walked to the plate, took one strike, and called it on himself before the umpire did; then another; then pointed to right-center field bleachers where he intended to hit the next pitch. And that is exactly what he did. But the whole incident was shrouded in caustic name-calling, initiated by words of contention. In the heat of controversy wild accusations are often flung out which have no ground in truth, leaving lingering and bitter regrets.

Lack of cooperation. Contention can gum up the works in Christian organizations and become the fly in the ointment of cooperative endeavors. An old Greek fable tells of a contest between the north wind and the sun to see which was stronger. Pointing to a man walking below, the sun said, "Why do we talk in vain? See that fellow? Whichever can take off his coat first is victor." The north wind agreed, then proceeded to do his best to doff the man's coat. He blew and blew, fumed, fussed, and fretted, but the man only pulled his coat all the more tightly around him. When the wind stopped blowing, the sun came and shone so warmly that the man, heated, took off his coat. The cooperation of Christian groups can be secured by winsome affability but can also be quickly destroyed by contentious nagging.

Divisions. A rough reply to the plea of the people to reduce taxes after the death of Solomon resulted in a divided kingdom. This contentious speech led to a permanent split between the Northern Kingdom, Israel, and the Southern Kingdom, Judah, punctuated in the ensuing two centuries by strife.

In a little Connecticut church a lady sat in morning worship, holding an infant in her arms. The baby, beginning to cry, was not easily quieted. Suddenly from the gallery struck out a rough, insulting voice, "Give the calf more rope!" The damage of that impulsive, wild remark caused the church heavy casualties. Ladies with infants left the church and joined a nearby smaller meeting place, where their babies could cry without being called calves.

Many a church has been divided by a contentious word. Church factions have gone so far as to line up in party fashion on voted issues. A split in a Dallas church, so serious that it was heard in both civil and denominational courts, began at a church dinner when an elder made a belligerent remark just because he received a smaller slice of ham than the child seated next to him.

Not only churches but friendships may be ended through contention. Barnabas and Paul, co-laborers of years' standing and co-founders of churches on Paul's first missionary journey, were divided by contention over the inclusion of Mark on the second journey.

David prayed to be kept from the strife of tongues (Ps. 31:20).

A CURE OF CONTENTION: SOFT WORDS

Commanded in Scripture. By nature man wants to keep chewing on the bone of contention. Strife, wrangling, insult, provocative speech, bitterness, wrath, clamor, abusiveness—all are forbidden in Scripture as fruits of a depraved heart (Rom. 1:29-32; 2 Cor. 12:20; Gal. 5:19-21, 26; Eph. 4:31; Titus 3:2).

But the new nature, inwrought by the Holy Spirit, transforms a man into a peace-loving brother, living amicably with fellow believers. "By this shall all men know that ye are My disciples, if ye have love one to another" (John 13:35). Contention is contrary to Christian character and behavior.

"Blessed are the peacemakers: for they shall be called the children of God" (Matt. 5:9).

"If it be possible . . . live peaceably with all men" (Rom. 12:18).

"Not rendering . . . railing for railing; but contrariwise blessing" (1 Peter 3:9).

"Be at peace among yourselves" (1 Thes. 5:13).

The pattern of many biblical saints. The supreme example is Christ who, when vehemently accused by the chief priests and scribes, answered not a word. "Prophesy who struck Thee," they taunted as they hit Him on the cheek. They mocked Him, arrayed Him in regal attire, reviled Him. "If Thou be the Son of God, come down from the cross." But He never reviled in return. Instead He begged, "Father, forgive them; for they know not what they do." Peter specifically stated that Christ was our example in this matter (1 Peter 2:21-23).

When stones were pelting Stephen's body so that he fell bruised and broken, he cried out, "Lord, lay not this sin to their charge."

Gideon went to war against the Midianites without asking help of the Ephraimites until the battle was nearly over. When the Ephraimites angrily asked Gideon why he hadn't called them when he first went to fight, Gideon answered their contentious words with a soft reply, pointing out that they had done far more than he. He could as easily have given a retort which would have touched off fireworks, but his soft answer abated their anger.

When David was sent with food to his brothers who were in the army fighting the Philistines, he heard the giant Goliath defying the armies of Israel and inquired why no one went to fight him. Immediately his eldest brother, Eliab, accused David of pride, naughtiness, and neglect of the sheep in the wilderness. David could have fought back but instead quietly asked, "What have I now done? Is there not a cause?" (1 Sam. 17:29) David won not only a victory over Goliath later, but he also won a victory over his own spirit by controlling it, even as the proverb says, "He that is slow to anger is better than the mighty; and he that ruleth his spirit than he that taketh a city" (Prov. 16:32).

Even Michael the archangel, when contending with the devil over the body of Moses, didn't dare bring against him a railing accusation but said, "The Lord rebuke thee" (Jude 9).

Stops argument. Since a gentle reply indicates that the party replying will not engage in battle, no fight can ensue; a genuine argument demands two opponents. No boxer enters the ring without an opponent to fight, nor does a crowd gather to watch a fighter shadowbox with himself. When Charles Haddon Spurgeon was still a boy preacher, he was warned about an overbearing woman who had threatened to give him a tongue lashing. Not long after, she met Spurgeon and let loose a flood of abuse. He smiled, "Yes, thank you, I am quite well. I hope you are the same."

This brought on another burst of vituperations only in a higher-pitched voice, to which, still smiling, he replied, "Yes, it does look as if it might rain. I think I'd better be going on."

"Bless me," she replied, "he's as deaf as a post. No use storming at him." And so her railings at Spurgeon ceased. We should discern when to answer, and when not to answer a fool according to his folly (Prov. 26:4-5). The publication *Chestnuts* contained this item, "The real art of conversation is not only to say the right thing in the right place but to leave unsaid the wrong thing at the tempting moment."

The difference between a successful marriage and a mediocre one often consists of leaving three or four things a day unsaid, according to marriage counselors.

How significant that "keep silent" is also translated "keep peace." For to keep silent or answer softly is to maintain peace. No answer, as well as a soft one, can sometimes turn away wrath. The power to wage verbal warfare usually resides in the kind of answer we give. Someone facetiously has said, "Keep your temper. Do not quarrel with an angry person but give him a soft answer. It is commanded by Holy Writ, and furthermore, it makes him madder than anything else you could say." This is not usually true. "A soft answer turneth away wrath."

A reckless woman drove at foolhardy speed, honking her horn and passing other cars on curves and hills. Suddenly a truck loomed in her path and only the skill of its driver averted a head-on collision. In ominous silence the truck driver got down from his cab and stalked toward the reckless driver. She expected a well-deserved tongue lashing, but without a word the truck driver poked his head through the window and with one finger sketched a circle above her head. "Lady," he whispered hoarsely "that's the way angels are made." Again he circled her head with an imaginary halo and with dignity went his way. The natural inclination under such a circumstance would be to lash out with the tongue, but the truck driver's soft answer probably prevented an ugly scene.

The manager of a department store was asked why he had such a shy, retiring girl at the complaint desk. "Why, I think you would need a bold, hard-boiled person there!" He answered, "Perhaps it does seem strange to have a girl that seems so gentle to handle the complaining, angry customers, but I tell you that's the kind of girl to put there. I have tried capable, hustling girls. But, you see, the average comer to the complaint desk is not trying to cheat the store. Most are irritated. They blame the store. They want to speak their minds, and if a hard-boiled girl explains that they are in the wrong, it only tangles things up and makes them angrier than ever. Now this gentle kind of girl does not explain except in a hesitating way. She looks shy and troubled as they talk, and 9 times out of 10 before the complaint is finished, the customer calms down and is ashamed of being angry. Why, I have seen women go to that desk so angry that they could hardly talk and end up saying, 'Never mind; it may have been partly my fault, and I'm sure you will fix it right.' The girl straightens them out in her gentle way. Oh, it's a great scheme. I hit on it by accident. I had no other girl to put there one week. But I'll never go back to the other kind of girl. No sir!"

When a door squeaks, use a little oil. When an exasperating situation confronts you, pour a little oil on troubled waters.

Requires time to think. How many things would remain unsaid if we only exercised a few moments' reflection before their utterance. To give a soft answer requires time, which in turn gives a check to the tongue. We should think twice before speaking once.

Very often people spring in anger at insignificant matters and sometimes in the midst of controversy do not know what they are arguing about. A newspaper cartoon showed Willy saying, "'Tis! 'Tis! 'Tis! 'Tis!" His pal just as emphatically retaliated, " 'Tisn't! 'Tisn't! 'Tisn't! 'Tisn't!"

Willie's mother inquired, " 'Tis! 'Tisn't! what?"

The boys, with blank looks on their faces, confessed, "We forgot!"

A young lawyer found a solution to the bickering among his children. He explained to them how a case is brought to court with a complaint filed by one person and a defense filed by another, followed by verbal argument at a trial. He suggested that children settle their quarrels in a similar manner. The children responded with great interest. The wisdom of the young lawyer's scheme soon became apparent, for when the children tried to reduce their grievances to paper, they usually saw that the complaint was too slight to merit their father's attention. If people would think grudges through, the chances are that points of contention which seem large would dissipate into insignificance.

Some people will say that it is just as bad to think a thing as to say it. However, many thoughts are better left unsaid. Lots of thoughts—as about others' dress or personal traits—if uttered would result in contention and resentment. The formulation of a soft answer helps us to think things through and leave unsaid the unnecessary.

Soon after buying a spacious farm, the new owner was warned that his nearest neighbor thought the property line intruded several feet on his territory. The new owners bristled. His first reaction was to stand up for his property rights. But then he gave it some thought. Not long later he met the neighbor, who asked, "Have you bought this place?"

"Yes."

"Well, sir, you've bought a lawsuit too. I claim your fence down there is 10 feet on my side of the line, and I'm going to take the matter to court and prove it."

The newcomer said, "Oh, no, don't do that. If the fence is on your side of the line, we'll just take it down and move it to where you think it should be."

"Do you mean that?"

"Of course I do," was the answer.

"Then," said the man, "that fence stays just where it is."

A soft answer not only turns away wrath but sometimes it breaks barriers.

SEVEN

TO TELL THE TRUTH

In March 1982 a Congressional page stated that he had had sex with two Congressmen who propositioned him, and that he had arranged a liaison between a senator and a homosexual prostitute. Five months later the 18-year-old page said at a news conference, "These allegations are not true. I have lied and I regret that." He expressed remorse for what he had done to the members of Congress, their families, Congressional staff members, and his own family. Some months before, this page had failed part of a polygraph test, administered by the FBI, but had then still insisted on the truth of his accusations.

In an article on the increasing use of lie detectors, the *Wall Street Journal* (10/16/84) reported that a New York retailer keeps a polygraph on hand and routinely tests some workers. An Indianapolis store tests job applicants and periodically checks managers with keys to the store. Also Caesar's World uses the detectors extensively at its Las Vegas club.

Lying ranks high among the vices of mankind. A University of Virginia psychologist reported, "People tell about two lies a day, or at least that is how many they will admit to" (*New York Times*, 2/12/85, p. C-8). Despite its prevalence, lying is a sin. "Lying lips are abomination to the Lord" (Prov. 12:22). Though many regard lies as harmless slips of speech, among seven items God hates, two refer to lying (Prov. 6:16-19), "a lying tongue" and "a false witness." Paul says, "Lie not one to another, seeing that ye have put off the old man with his deeds" (Col. 3:9). The ninth commandment reads, "Thou shalt not bear false witness."

WHAT IS A LIE?

A simple definition of lying is saying that which is not true with intent to deceive.

Kidding is not lying. One April 1st a lady received a phone call from her sister to go into the kitchen to look for an article supposedly left there. After a brief search failed to locate the object, the lady returned to the phone to hear, "April Fool." Her sister was jesting, not lying.

A mistake in a statement is not a lie. When a broadcaster announces that 20 people were killed in a plane crash, and the number turns out to be 19, he is reporting erroneous information, but he is not lying for there is no intent to deceive.

Polite formalities should not be classified as lies. When an acquaintance asks you how you are, and you reply, "Fine, thank you," though you have a nagging headache, your answer should not be considered a lie, for passing neighbors are not too interested in the state of your health. That reply is just part of a cultural ritual.

Action contrary to one's previous statement is not lying, when unforeseen circumstances lead one to alter his previous intent.

Though Peter at first said to Christ, "Thou shalt never wash my feet," a few words from Jesus caused Peter to beg Him to wash not only his feet, but also his hands and head (John 13:6-9).

It is no lie to conceal or withhold part of the truth when it is not expedient or necessary to tell it. When Samuel was commanded by the Lord to annoint as king, a son of Jesse, Samuel said, "How can I go? If Saul hear it, he will kill me. And the Lord said, Take an heifer with thee, and say, I am come to sacrifice to the Lord" (1 Sam. 16:2). Saul had no right to know the entire purpose of Samuel's mission to Jesse, nor was Samuel under obligation to reveal it. Concealment by Samuel was not lying.

How intolerable life would be if we were required to disclose all the truth we know. Withholding truth is often both necessary and kind. "A talebearer revealeth secrets; but he that is of a faithful spirit concealeth the matter" (Prov. 11:13).

Probably the most knotty problem relating to lying has to do with telling a lie to do good, such as saving someone's life. A Gestapo agent has come to search a house in which a Jewish wife is hiding, and at the door asked the husband if anyone is inside. Should he tell the soldier the truth and get her killed, or should he lie to save her life? This ethical area is sometimes called "the tragic moral choice." The two major schools of thought on this problem are known as "the greater good" and "the lesser evil" theories.

When Rahab lied about the whereabouts of the spies, to save their lives, according to "the greater good" school of thought she was doing right, for saving a life is more important than telling the truth. The saving of a life not only annuls the lower law against lying, but makes the telling of the lie a good. In fact, according to this view, to tell the truth would be morally wrong, for it would be abetting murder.

Those who hold the other view, though commending Rahab

for her action in saving the spies, insist that the New Testament commends her solely for her faith in receiving the spies and sending them out another way, and does not express approval for her lie. According to this "lesser of two evils" theory, Rahab is commended not because of her lying, but in spite of it. Calvin terms Rahab's act not devoid of the praise of virtue, but not spotlessly pure. According to this view a lie is never justifiable. However, both theories agree that when the alternatives of saving a life or lying confront us, the loving choice is to save the life. If lying in this case is evil, God will grant forgiveness. As Peter says, "Charity [love] shall cover the multitude of sins" (1 Peter 4:8).

WAYS OF LYING

The book *Do You Lie with Finesse?* carried this subcaption: "The Complete Alibi Handbook will teach you to be a perfect liar and will give you an 'out' for almost every situation." What a variety of ways there are to lie!

Direct lie. When Cain answered God's question as to murdered Abel's whereabouts with "I know not," that was a straight lie. Joseph's brothers lied to their father when they pled ignorance as to whether or not the blood-stained coat they brought back belonged to their missing brother. When blind Isaac asked Jacob, "Who art thou, my son?" Jacob answered, "I am Esau thy firstborn." No answer could have been more calculated to deceive.

Professional lying. A newspaper article told of a lady in California who for $6 would come up with "a little white lie" to get a buyer out of a sticky situation. A more complicated excuse cost more. If you're in trouble with your boss about missing work, so there's just no way you can take another day off, she'll get on the phone and say, "I'm nurse so-and-so from such-and-such a hospital,'' and ask whoever answers the phone to tell you that you left your glasses, or wallet, or whatever at the hospital. She's played a lot of roles on the phone, including counselor, police dispatcher, and receptionist. Before making a call, she cooks up a script, scans it for possible snags, then talks so rapidly that there's no time for questions. (*Journal-News,* Feb. 8, 1985).

Perjury. A formal lie—a false statement under oath in court—constitutes perjury. Great pains were taken in Old Testament times to see that testimony was reliable and true. Two witnesses were necessary.

Social lying. ''Sorry, I have another meeting I have to attend tomorrow''—the fictional, fabricated previous engagement—admittedly does help life run more smoothly as well as prevent hurt feelings. But God said a false witness should not go unpunished, but should receive a penalty for his false witness (Deut. 19:16-19).

Half-truths. It's possible to give part of the truth, but at the same time tell a half-lie. On two different occasions Abraham said that Sarah was his sister so as to protect her from possible harm. This was partly truth, for she was his half sister; but it was partly false, for she was also his wife. Isaac did the same with Rebekah who, though distantly related to him, was not his real sister.

Double meaning. It's possible to lie by using right words but with ambiguity. A preacher stopped at a fish market after a week of fruitless fishing. ''Throw me a dozen of those mackerel—one by one. I've got to say I caught them, and I can't lie about it!''

Mental reservation. A person may lie through mental maneuvering. A knock at the door or a ring of the phone causes mother to say, ''If it's for me, I'm not in.'' She explains, ''I'm not in to that particular party.'' Someone said, ''Little white lies soon become double features in technicolor.''

Quoting out of context. A speaker said, "I like Canada better than the U.S. with respect to Sunday observance." He was quoted as saying, "I like Canada better than the U.S.," giving an entirely different meaning. Caution should be exercised to quote the remarks of others correctly, especially those with whom one disagrees.

Self-detraction. Mock humility about one's abilities or achievements is sometimes uttered to secure a contradiction which feeds this vanity. A high schooler says, "I'm a poor student," when his grades are all As and Bs. He makes this understatement because he wants to hear someone say, "You're a smart student. You get good grades."

Flattery. Someone said, "A flatterer is one who says things to your face that he wouldn't say behind your back." An old proverb puts it, "Ninety-four percent of soft soap is lye." Says Psalmist David, "With flattering lips and with a double heart do they speak. The Lord shall cut off all flattering lips" (Ps. 12:23). A flattering tongue brings ruin (Prov. 26:28). Few things are more potent for harm than flattery because such remarks are readily welcomed, carefully treasured, and encourage undertakings beyond one's competence.

Exaggeration. Pupils were asked to construct a sentence using the word *amphibious.* A fisherman's son suggested, "Most fish stories am fibious."

A young man, returning from a football game in a car with four others, stopped to see his uncle, who lived in a little mining town along the way. It was pitch-dark. As he got out of the car, he nearly walked into a lady. He apologized but she began to scream and then ran. His uncle was out, so the young man climbed in the car and the five lads drove away. He wanted to go to the police and explain, but his companions advised against it. When a friend from that town visited the young man two weeks later, he told how a large crowd had gathered in front of his uncle's house that night. When the police came, the lady told how a man grabbed her, swore, and tried to force her into a car full of men. A lady living nearby claimed she saw it all from her window, vouching for the facts. Such exaggeration is lying.

It's possible to exaggerate the attendance at a church service, the size of a church budget, or the number of conversions from a crusade. A religious paper reported that several people had been converted in an evangelistic campaign, implying numerous professions, when in reality only two conversions were recorded.

Pragmatic lies. Pragmatism, a philosophy of temporal expediency, says that whatever works is right. A lie isn't wrong, except when you're caught, according to this view. A young man in America wrote his missionary parents in Africa that he attended church faithfully every Sunday. The truth was that he rarely went to church, but he knew his lie would make them happy.

After a sermon on "Archeology and the Bible," a skeptic told a skeptic friend the talk was very unconvincing, but later that evening, meeting a Bible-believing friend, told him that the sermon almost made a believer out of him. The Bible speaks against double-tonguedness, telling one thing to one person, and a different thing to another. A proverb says, "Keep not two tongues in one mouth."

At halftime with his team losing, Knute Rockne, famous Notre Dame football coach who always had a bag of tricks up his sleeve to win games, choked up his players when he read them a telegram from his six-year-old son, "I want daddy's team to win."

Rockne commented, "Boys, that youngster of mine is lying sick in a hospital right now in South Bend. He's a mighty sick lad, and I promised to bring him home the football as a present. Are you men going to let the kid down?" Though they took a terrific pounding, they won the game, all for the sick lad. As they walked wearily off the field, who should meet them but a perfectly healthy six-year-old, waving a Notre Dame banner and yelling, "Hooray! My pop's team won!"

Business. A used-car salesman waited on a customer who had picked out a certain car which the saleman knew was in poor condition. The customer asked to be driven home in the car. The salesman marveled that the car performed so well. At his home the customer pulled out his pen and started to sign the purchase papers, then halted, "One question, sir. If you were me, would you buy this car?"

The salesman's heart did a flip-flop. He was broke and needed the commission. While inwardly debating, he looked up and there on the customer's wall was a motto, "God hears every word you say." There was no sale.

Advertising. A book subtitled "The Inside Truth about Advertising" gives many examples of tricks of the trade, involving misleading headlines and distorted TV commercials. For example, a leading meat packer advertised, "One pound of our franks is as nourishing as one pound of steak." But asks the author, "Did you ever try eating ten frankfurters in a pound package—at one meal?" Ads for a hair conditioner stated, "Actually makes your hair feel stronger." A dermatologist commented, "This is advertising nonsense. Scientifically it's baseless."

Years ago the *Detroit News* carried an ad on page 23 in which baseball's home-run star of that decade, Hank Greenberg, said, "You can't beat Raleighs for less nicotine . . . less throat irritants . . . all-round safer smoking. I recommend Raleighs to all my friends." In an interview on page 17 of the same issue Hank Greenberg said, "The doctors said I had a stomach disorder and I'm giving up cigarettes and coffee. I never was much of a smoker anyway. I'm sleeping better now and I feel much better."

Lies to God. Ananias was asked, "Why hath Satan filled thine heart to lie to the Holy Ghost?" (Acts 5:3) Unkept vows to God are lies. People vow to attend church regularly, serve faithfully, attend prayer meetings, but fail to keep their word to God. We should follow the example of Hannah who kept her vow to give back to God any child He might loan her (1 Sam. 1:10).

THE MISCHIEF OF LYING

Lying affects us. A clerk weighed the only chicken left in an ice-packed barrel, and announced, "Five pounds." When the customer said he wanted a bigger one, the clerk put the chicken back in the barrel, then pulled the same chicken out. Putting it on the scales and adding pressure, the clerk announced, "Seven pounds."

"That's fine," replied the customer, "I'll take both of them."

Lying eventually catches up with us, as in the case of the girl who took 10 days off work, pretending to have the flu. Then she really caught the bug and had to work while actually ill in order to cover up her lie. "It was awful," she moaned.

Lying affects the liar. Since we were meant to possess truth in the inward parts, lying lowers self-respect. In addition, if we persist, our credibility will be doubted. Also, one lie leads to another till we become hopelessly tangled in the octopus of deceit. As Mark Twain put it, "If you tell the truth, you don't have to remember anything."

Lying affects others. Lying disrupts the fabric of society which operates on a supposed foundation of truth. If a person turned on his TV to watch a 9 P.M. program, only to find the program had just ended, what havoc a continued practice of this would create, especially if deliberately done by the TV guide. Or, if people arrived at the airport for the 7 P.M. jet to Los Angeles, to discover it wouldn't leave till midnight, a steady diet of such timetable deceptions would soon confuse the public into a hopeless lack of confidence.

Lying also leads others to think that truth is unimportant. If parents lie, can they complain if their children do likewise? A little girl who hears her mother say, "Oh, here come those horrid neighbors to visit us," then hears her mother greet them, "Oh, hello, do come in. I was just wishing you would pay us a visit," would not surprise us if she later practiced duplicity.

James Boswell, biographer of Samuel Johnson, recorded how the latter, because he did not want his servant to lie, would retreat to the attic without mentioning it to his servant, so if anyone called, the servant could honestly say he didn't know where his master was. Johnson reasoned thus, "If I allow my servant to tell a lie for me, don't I have reason to expect that he will tell many lies himself?"

Lying sometimes convicts the wrong man. It helped to crucify Christ and stone Stephen, for false witnesses testified at both trials.

Lying affects our relationship with God. Lying not only harms the one who lies and upsets society, but it also affects our relationship with God. Habitual lying may indicate we are not God's child but rather under the sway of Satan who "is a liar, and the father of" lies (John 8:44). Lying is contradictory to God's nature, for He is truth.

Lying, unless forgiven, will keep us from heaven. After the glorious picture of the New Jerusalem (Rev. 21) comes a warning that into that city shall not enter "anything that defileth, neither whatsoever worketh abomination, or maketh a lie" (v. 27). Again in the last chapter of the Bible we're told, "For without are dogs, and sorcerers, and whoremongers, and murderers, and idolaters, and whosoever loveth and maketh a lie" (22:15).

We must recognize the sinfulness of our lives which helped nail Christ to the cross, and ask Him to forgive us through His redeeming sacrifice. Then, as God's children, we'll have His indwelling Spirit to enable us to keep this New Testament command, "Wherefore putting away lying, speak every man truth with his neighbor" (Eph. 4:25).

Don Landaas, a member of the elite Marine Ceremonial Guard, was on helicopter guard detail at Camp David in May 1959, the weekend President Eisenhower was entertaining England's Prime Minister Macmillan. Doing what he shouldn't have, he slid back the door of Eisenhower's helicopter, sat down, and began to pray. Superior officers of the guard happened to be checking at the moment, caught him off his post, arrested him, and sent him back to the guardhouse in Washington for disciplinary action.

His buddies advised him to say he thought he had heard a noise in the helicopter and was investigating. But he prayed for strength to tell the truth at his court-martial.

On the day of the trial, Landaas stood before a colonel and 10 other officers. After the charges were read, the colonel asked Landaas if he had anything to say for himself.

Replied Landaas, "Colonel, I should like to tell the truth. That night at Camp David I didn't go into the helicopter because I heard anything. I went in there because I wanted to pray. As a Christian I have dedicated myself to my Master just as you, a colonel in the Marine Corps, are a man dedicated to your commander."

The colonel replied, "Landaas, I believe you, but I have no alternative but to punish you. Had someone slipped up by the side of the helicopter when you were inside and poured water in the gas tank, you might have been responsible for the President's death."

Landaas was sentenced to 20 days hard labor, fined $50, and busted from first class to buck private. Said the colonel, "Your court-martial removes your top secret clearance so you can no longer guard the President." But because of his otherwise fine record, the imprisonment was suspended and he was given a choice of duties.

Two weeks later, Landaas, an accomplished accordian player, had an audition with the Marine Band, and was appointed accordion soloist for the last two years of his military hitch.

Comments Landaas, who in recent years has given musical performances in many churches and Bible conferences, "I saw that telling the truth is the only course for a Christian to follow. As a member of the Marine Band I started out as a sergeant. I sewed three stripes on the arm from which one had been removed two weeks before. Three months later, when Eisenhower returned to Camp David for his weekend talks with Khrushchev, I was one of six musicians chosen to go along to provide the music. I returned to Camp David, a place I had been told I would never set foot in again. I flew up in one of the same helicopters I had previously guarded, along with the one I had prayed in and had been arrested in. I met President Eisenhower, spoke with him, played for him and in the following months for 20 other heads of state. It pays to tell the truth."

EIGHT
ARE YOU A LITTERBUG?

I t is said that Will Rogers never told a vulgar story. Asked to repeat an off-color story he had just heard, he replied, "I'll have to wait three days before I can tell it. It'll take that long to launder it."

Of another speaker who had related a suggestive story, Rogers remarked, "Judging by the story my friend told, I guess his mind is like a race horse—it runs best on a dirt track."

Paul wrote to the Ephesians, "But fornication, and all uncleanness, or covetousness, let it not be once named among you, as becometh saints; neither filthiness, nor foolish talking, nor jesting, which are not convenient; but rather giving of thanks" (Eph. 5:3-4).

IS IT WRONG TO JOKE?
Many Christians conclude from this text that all joking is wrong and humor must be avoided. Consequently, some Christians

have faces long enough to lick spaghetti out of the bottom of a barrel. Little June was visiting her grandparents' farm. Grandfather, a very religious man, tolerated no merriment. Seeking relief from the depressive gloom, the little girl wandered out to the barn, where she spied a donkey. Noting the sad look on its long face, she dolefully said as she patted it, "Poor donkey, you got Grandpa's religion too."

A deacon was meeting the visiting preacher at the train. He had never met him, but selecting a likely looking fellow from the crowd, asked, "Are you the minister?"

"No," came the gruff reply. "It's my indigestion that makes me look like this."

Some condemn joking by saying that Jesus never laughed and that Paul forbade jesting. If this text should be so interpreted, then no laugh of ours must ever ring again, no word of wit ever pass our lips, no smile ever cross our faces. All joke columns would be wrong. What a drab world this would be!

Humor is a gift from God; it has its own place. "God must have meant us to laugh," someone has said, "else He wouldn't have made so many parrots, mules, monkeys, and human beings." Words can refresh a tired mind, just as exercise or rest relaxes a tired body. Words of humor that relax the mind are not wrong.

Volumes have been written on humor. For example, even Aristotle in his *Nicomachean Ethics* spoke of a ready wit as the proper median between boorishness and buffoonery. Sigmund Freud wrote hundreds of pages on wit. Carolyn Wells has a book titled *Outline of Humor*. Stephen Leacock wrote on *The Greatest Pages of American Humor*. Henri Bergson's *Laughter* has been termed an important text on the subject. Wit is usually described as the defining of similarities in dissimilarities, or sense in nonsense, or the discovery of incongruity. One painstaking German student traced the history of humor back to eleven original joke patterns or situations. Humor is human. God meant for us to laugh.

Job told his comforters, "Ye are the people, and wisdom shall die with you" (Job 12:2). Jesus' teachings have lots of wit, like the man with a tree trunk protruding from his eye condemning a fellow for having a tiny sliver in his eye. Jesus spoke of straining at a gnat and then swallowing a camel, and a camel going through the eye of a needle, and of a man who, forgiven a debt of 10,000 talents ($10 million), failed to forgive a fellow servant who owed him 100 denarii ($15).

Christian leaders have always enjoyed good humor. Spurgeon's lectures to his students contain many funny stories. Moody enjoyed hearing a good story at the end of a day's work and would sit back and laugh hilariously.

Humor can play a part in Christian work. It helped win a noted missionary. A young man wandered into one of Moody's English campaign meetings, where a minister was making an unusually long prayer. Moody burst out, "While that good brother is finishing his prayer, we'll sing a hymn." The thoughtless young man had intended to stay just a few minutes but, captivated by this sanctified humor, remained and was converted. He became the father of Labrador missions, none other than Sir William Grenfell.

Humor can also be used to illustrate truth; it is often an effective teaching device. One well-known teacher, skilled in its use, said in defense of humor, "While their mouths are open in laughter, I pour down a good dose of old-fashioned truth."

The text does not forbid all jesting. One authority says, "There is no reason to suppose that the apostle meant to condemn all play of humor, which is a divine gift and which in moderation has its own useful place as a means of refreshing the spirit" (*Pulpit Commentary on Ephesians*, p. 208).

IMPROPER JESTING

Some jesting is wrong. What a man laughs at indicates his moral nature. Professor J. Alexander Findlay pointed out, "Even the kind of jokes we make reveals our character more than our set speeches." Pleasantries are all right, but "meaneries" are wrong.

Making fun of a person's handicaps. "Thou shalt not curse the deaf, nor put a stumbling block before the blind" (Lev. 19:14). It is wrong to make fun of others' disabilities.

Making fun of another's appearance. Young men mocked Elisha, "Go up, thou bald head; go up, thou bald head" (2 Kings 2:23). And two bears came out of the wood and tore 42 of those who mocked.

Making fun of another's misfortune. Mother found Junior crying. "What's the matter, Dear?"

"Daddy hit his thumb with a hammer," said Junior.

"You shouldn't cry over that; you should laugh!"

"I did laugh," whimpered Junior.

Says the wise man, "Whoso mocketh the poor reproacheth his Maker" (Prov. 17:5). A circuit-riding preacher of a century ago stopped at a farmhouse for some refreshment. He was offered bread and milk and an iron spoon. Returning to the city, he jokingly mentioned the meal and remarked, "And an iron spoon is a bit heavy on the meal." His friends laughed with him. He meant no harm, but in due time the joke traveled many miles, back to the rural farmhouse.

"I regret the preacher had fun at our expense," said the lady of the remote farm. "Had we been more prosperous we would have been able to provide a silver spoon. We could only give him the best we had. We are sorry he failed to understand."

Receiving this reaction a week later, the preacher hurried to the barn, saddled his horse, mounted, and rode through a rainstorm some 50 miles to offer his humble apologies.

> I don't object to laughter—
> It has its proper place—
> But, when I'm the object of it,
> I don't like it in my face!
> —Author unknown

Making fun of a person's name. Punning on a proper name is poor humor, even in fun.

Jests of drunken revelry. The silly remarks of the intoxicated are in poor taste. Revelings that issue in noisy vulgarities dishonor God.

IRREVERENT HUMOR

Serious truths should not be treated lightly. A public studio audience was warmed up before its weekly network telecast by an announcer who invariably told a joke about hell that made everyone roar with laughter. If hell is a real place, as Christ taught, then it's no laughing matter.

How easily our familiarity with holy topics can slip into flippancy. Some smilingly assert, "Oh, I'll get around to it when the Spirit moves me," a careless reference to the third Person of the Trinity. Students about to graduate from Christian schools have jokingly remarked, "Oh, I'll graduate, the Dean willing," a saucy substitution for "the Lord willing."

Humor plunged to the depths when Jesus became the target of scorn. Abusive soldiers asked Him, "Prophesy unto us, Thou Christ: Who is he that smote Thee?" (Matt. 26:68) Robing Him in scarlet, they fitted a crown of thorns on His head, placed a reed in His right hand, and bowing mocked Him, "Hail, King of the Jews" (27:29).

One skeptic sneered, as he waited impatiently in a hotel, "This elevator is as slow as the second coming of Christ."

Ridicule of this precious doctrine was foretold by Peter: "Knowing this first, that there shall come in the last days scoffers, walking after their own lusts, and saying, Where is the promise of His coming? For since the fathers fell asleep, all things continue as they were from the beginning of the Creation" (2 Peter 3:3-4).

Admittedly, Bible and humor can be mingled appropriately without belittling the sacred Word. But care must be exercised so as not to quote Bible verses to point up a jest. Dr. Isaac Page, late deputy secretary of the China Inland Mission, was extremely fond of jokes, but had definite convictions against mixing Scripture and humor. At a dinner he heard the question asked, "Who will go out and get the bread?" Then Page heard a voice reply, "Here am I; send me." Page immediately demanded, "Who said that?"

Meekly a young college girl owned up. He gave her a sermonette which was never forgotten by the girl who came to hold a responsible position in a Christian college. When verses are used tritely or thoughtlessly, their serious edge may be dulled for later encounter. The same caution ought to be used with hymns, lest their sacred import be forever blunted.

When a well-known actor played God in a popular movie, his words which represented God speaking qualified as sacreligious.

IMMORAL SUGGESTIVENESS

Let's look at the real meaning of the word "jesting" in Ephesians 5:4. "Filthiness" has to do with one's whole life; we are to avoid impurity. "Foolish talking" has to do with empty, idle conversation. But what does "jesting" mean?

The word translated "jesting" means versatility or aptness in turning. It implies nimbleness of wit in turning conversation into another channel, mixing conversation of double meanings, quick innuendos, and smart repartee. It is suggestiveness along certain lines.

Cameron Orr, for many years a missionary on the Welland Canal, used his ability at turning conversation into a definite channel. For eight months of the year Orr boarded boats as they slowly passed through the locks of the 27-mile canal, left Christian literature, and spoke briefly to the sailors. He had to work rapidly so he developed an aptness at turning a conversation into a Gospel witness. Before long he would get a word in for Jesus by taking some remark of a sailor, or some item familiar to sailors, and get in a plug for biblical truth.

For example, meeting a sailor working on a different vessel, he heard the lad remark, "In this work you're liable to be on one boat one day and another the next."

"Yes," Orr answered, "it's here today and gone tomorrow. But if gone tomorrow, where will you be?"

Meeting another sailor for the first time, he heard the fellow apologize, "My hands are dirty, or I'd shake."

"Oh, don't worry about dirty hands. It's a dirty heart I'm after. Tell me, will soap take that dirt off?"

"No, sir. It takes a special compound."

"I've a special compound for dirt on the heart—the blood of Christ."

He sometimes used this approach: "When the good ship 'Gospel' sails for the eternal port, I want you to be on deck. The good ship 'Gospel' is still calling people to come aboard."

To the steward he began, "Your job and mine are similar— feeding people, and a thankless task at that."

To the first mate he said, "You need the captain, but he can only help a little. You need the Captain above."

His versatility won the cooperation of a stiff captain with whom he found it difficult to speak. Once in Orr's presence the captain ordered the mate to "drop the spear pole."

"What use is a spear pole, sir?" asked Orr.

"To point me the way, to drop me on the course."

"You know, sir, John the Baptist was a spear pole, pointing men and women to Christ. Every time you drop the spear pole remember, 'He must increase, but I must decrease.' " This took the captain off his guard and won his friendship.

Orr often said, "We're all sailing the sea of life. There are two ports—heaven and hell. If you let Jesus come aboard, it will be heaven and not hell."

Cameron Orr possessed versatility or aptness in turning a conversation into another channel. Is this what is forbidden in Ephesians 5:4? Was he violating Scripture by turning topics of conversation into spiritual and challenging channels? Not at all. A study of the context and the people to whom the command was written would clarify it for us.

Versatility in itself is not sin. But it is aptness at turning conversation into immoral lines that is wrong. Note the sequence: filthiness, foolish talking, jesting. Verse 3 speaks against "fornication, and all uncleanness, or covetousness" and verse 5 against one who is a "whoremonger . . . unclean person, [or] covetous." So it is jesting along immoral lines that is meant. Ephesus was noted for its shameless lust. Thus this command would be well understood, where on every street corner conversation would be turned into double meaning or suggestiveness and where talk was polluted with hidden sensual meaning. Not jesting per se, but jesting that is vulgar and vile, draws the apostle's censure. All stories that are obscene and ribald should be banished from our repertory. It was against such humor, the immoral, swashbuckling, and bawdy mirth of the Elizabethan stage, that the Puritans reacted so strongly. The twelfth verse states that it is a shame even to speak of those wicked things done in secret.

Ephesus isn't the only place where dirty jokes and suggestiveness are rampant. Our society is saturated with them. Popular songs often have double meanings. Some TV comedians delight in the indecent and indelicate. Joke columns contain offensive humor. Groups of youth, office workers, and people at parties tell filthy stories, then laugh hilariously. The New Testament plainly forbids "filthy communication out of your mouth" (Col. 3:8). The *Revised Standard Version* calls it "foul talk from your mouth."

At a staff meeting of youth workers the conversation began to drift toward the topic of homosexuality. Then it began to border on the risque. Suddenly one of the mature leaders let out a strong, firm command: "Change the subject!" Immediately the talk turned toward more elevating matters. Later the worker, asked if he had given the order on purpose replied, "Yes, the conversation was getting out of hand. The Bible says, 'Whatsoever things are pure . . . think on these things' (Phil. 4:8). That's what I was trying to get us to do. One of the Beatitudes says, 'Blessed are the pure in heart: for they shall see God' (Matt. 5:8). No Christian should tell an off-color story. Nor should he intentionally listen to one. If social pressure forbids walking away from the scene, a person can register his disapproval by not laughing. And when the chance comes, quietly but firmly say, 'I'm a Christian, and Jesus died that the world might be a better place. I don't believe dirty jokes contribute to that improvement.' If there had been only one dirty joke ever told in the world, Jesus Christ would still have had to die."

Sometimes people won't tell a certain story if a preacher is around. God's standard is the same whether or not a preacher is present. One day an officer in General Grant's army said, "I've a good story to tell; there are no ladies about."

Grant rebuked him, "There are gentlemen around, though." May we always remember that an ear which never closes listens to our every word.

L.L. Wightman, in *Rivers of Living Water,* tells how George Brown, on hearing the clatter of a wheelbarrow in front of his house, stepped to the window. Who could be wheeling a barrow, and with what could it be loaded? He had ordered nothing that would be delivered like that.

Well, of all things! Manley Strong, his wheelbarrow loaded with all manner of garbage, had turned into his yard and was approaching the front door. George Brown stared in amazement and wonder. What on earth was he doing out there with all that trash—rotten apples, tin cans, ashes, and what not?

The motley collection contrasted strongly with the neat lawn and beautiful flower beds, which were a source of great pride to the owner. Now that this load had nearly reached his front door, it took him but an instant to step outside to investigate.

"Good morning, Mr. Brown," Manley greeted him. "I've brought a load of garbage, and I'm wondering where on your lawn you wish to have it dumped."

George Brown's eyes opened wide with surprise, then anger. "Where on my lawn do I wish that stuff? Have you gone crazy? Do you see any signs telling you to dump garbage here?"

Manley pointed to a beautiful flower bed beside the porch. "There is room for it there," he suggested, ignoring the owner's sarcasm. "I really believe it is a good place to dump this load. One load surely would not make any difference."

George Brown gasped. He now knew the man was crazy or else was ridiculing him. "You dump that stuff here and see what happens," he threatened, considering that the farce had gone far enough.

"Would you prefer it in the middle of the lawn?" Manley asked.

"Say, what's the meaning of all this?" the irate owner asked. "The best thing you can do is to get that stuff out of here."

Manley nodded. "I really believe this stuff should be taken to the garbage dump,'' he agreed. ''But I thought if you could dump your garbage where you pleased, I certainly should have the same privilege.''

''What do you mean?'' George Brown asked.

''Let me refresh your memory. You'll understand what I mean in a minute. Do you remember talking yesterday afternoon with a group of lads? Yes, I know you do. And before you left them you dumped a foul story on them, and also some profane language. Two of those lads are in my Sunday School class. I spend time and effort to keep the lives of those boys pure and clean, and they are as much a source of pride to me as are your beautiful lawn and flower beds to you. Yet you did not hesitate to dump your foul garbage on the minds of those lads. Having done so, you laughed and went away, leaving your garbage there to breed evil thoughts and possibly evil deeds. Of course you do not wish your flowers buried beneath a pile of garbage; and neither do I wish the love and purity of those lads spoiled by your offensive stories and language.''

George Brown squirmed under the attack. Manley had so much truth on his side that nothing could be said in reply.

''You could remove this stuff from your lawn,'' Manley continued. ''But it is a more difficult thing to remove evil thoughts which have been sown in a life. Well, I guess I've said enough,'' Manley concluded. ''Good morning, Mr. Brown.''

And George Brown stood there speechless, as the wheelbarrow and its load clattered down the walk.

NINE
PATTING YOURSELF ON THE BACK

An ant climbed on an elephant's back and asked for a ride over a bridge. After they had crossed, the ant exclaimed, "My, but didn't we shake that bridge!"

The ant apparently did not possess the problem of low self-esteem. In a speech before the 1982 Evangelical Press Association convention (as reported in the *Evangelical Newsletter*) Hope College psychology teacher David Myers pointed out that a more common human error is not an inferiority complex, but a superiority complex. He reported that psychologists are amassing new data to back up the prevalence of pride. Myers said that several streams of study "merge to form a powerful river of evidence."

For example, people readily accept credit for their successes but blame their failures on external factors. "When I win at Monopoly it's because of my business acumen. When I lose, it's the throw of the dice."

Most people view themselves as better than average. When

high school seniors were asked to compare themselves with their peers, 60 percent regarded themselves better than average in athletic ability, but only 6 percent below average. In leadership ability, 70 percent rated themselves above average and only 2 percent under average. In ability to get along with others, zero percent of the 829,000 students who responded reported themselves below average, and 25 percent saw themselves in the top 1 percent.

At the University of Waterloo some students were exposed to a message about the value of frequent toothbrushing. Soon after, in a seemingly different experiment, the same students recalled brushing their teeth more often during the preceding two weeks than did those not exposed to the message. Apparently we make a habit of revising our past in order to preserve our positive self-evaluation.

Researchers have discovered that people overestimate the accuracy of their judgments. For example, though they don't expect a certain thing to happen, when it does, they boast, "I knew it all the time."

Other experiments show that most of us posssess unrealistic optimism. Students saw themselves as far more likely than their classmates to someday get a good job, draw a good salary, own a home, and far less likely to experience divorce, loss of job, or terminal illness.

When residents of an Indiana town were asked by phone to volunteer three hours to an American Cancer Society drive, only 4 percent agreed to do so. But when a similar group of other townsfolk were called and asked to predict how they would react to such a request, almost half prophesied they would help.

Jeremiah wrote, "The heart is deceitful above all things, and desperately wicked; who can know it?" (Jer. 17:9) Psalmist David suggests that no one can see his own errors (Ps. 19:12). All of the preceding research points to an overexalted view of ourselves, and all the inherent braggadocio. Such boastful blindness separates us from God and from each other. On the other hand, recognition of our pride can show our need of Christ, who can forgive us of our shortcomings and adopt us into His family, the real basis for positive self-esteem.

Paul's picture of depraved human nature includes the sin of boasting (Rom. 1:30). In the sins accentuated in the last days he also lists bragging (2 Tim. 3:2). The weeping Prophet Jeremiah says, "Thus saith the Lord, Let not the wise man glory in his wisdom, neither let the mighty man glory in his might, let not the rich glory in his riches; but let him that glorieth glory in this, that he understandeth and knoweth Me, that I am the Lord which exercise loving-kindness, judgment, and righteousness in the earth; for in these things I delight, saith the Lord" (Jer. 9:23-24). He indicates that there is a wrong type of boasting and a right type.

THE WRONG KIND OF BOASTING
Boasting of things known to be untrue. Making claims which cannot be substantiated is boasting. In addition, it involves lying. No shock results from learning that men of the world often make grandiose statements which are nothing but the products of their inflamed imaginations. But it is almost unbelievable that men who deal with the truth from behind the sacred desk should make grandiose, ungrounded claims.

Some years ago I interviewed for a feature article a man who boasted graduation from several schools, friendship with promi-nent theatrical people, connection with major radio networks, and performances in famous places, including the Metropolitan Opera. Investigation revealed flat contradiction to all his major claims. He later broke down and admitted his falsehoods to the magazine's editor. The article, needless to say, never saw the light of day.

Also painting one's past worse than it really was constitutes sin of a similar stripe. How tempting, in relating escapades of yesteryears, to add a little embellishment in order to make a more thrilling story! When next relating the same incident, how easy it is to include the addition as part of the truth. Before long our twisted natures enable us to believe with intense fervor in the actuality of all the accruements with which we have adorned our original stories.

"Why boasteth thou thyself in mischief, O mighty man?" (Ps. 52:1) Genuine shame for past misdeeds forbids relating such misdeeds, except under unusual circumstances, and then only with guarded reluctance. We may be sure that only with deep inward pain did Paul tell of his preconversion persecutions of the church of God. To exaggerate our evil deeds is to play with truth and make light of sin.

Boasting of things thought to be true. Boasting of some accomplishment, knowledge, or experience which is only imaginary, but thought to be real, is self-deception. "Whoso boasteth himself of a false gift is like clouds and wind without rain" (Prov. 25:14).

People often take credit for something they don't do or don't have and mention it in conversation in swaggering fashion. When some plan has been pushed to a successful conclusion, it is not uncommon to hear someone say, "That was my idea!" Often the idea was suggested by another or was the joint product of group discussion.

How easy it is for Americans to boast about their country as though its greatness is due to our industry and initiative. President Lincoln's proclamation in 1863, setting aside a day for national humiliation and prayer, is still relevant today: "Intoxicated with unbroken success, we have become too self-sufficient to feel the necessity of redeeming and preserving grace—too proud to pray to the God who made us.

"We have grown in numbers, wealth, and power, as no other nation has grown—but we have forgotten God.

"We have vainly imagined that all these blessings were produced by some superior virtue and wisdom of our own. It behooves us, then, to humble ourselves, to confess our national sins, and to pray for clemency and forgiveness."

Lincoln's proclamation reminds us of God's warning to Israel that when their flocks, silver, and gold multiplied, and they had lovely homes and good food, they were not to lift up their hearts and say, "My power and the might of mine hand hath gotten me this wealth. But thou shalt remember the Lord thy God; for it is He that giveth thee power to get wealth" (Deut. 8:17-18).

How many morally upright people think they possess standing with God, when in His sight all their supposed righteousness is as filthy rags. The Pharisee was certainly self-deceived when he boasted, "God, I thank Thee that I am not as other men are, extortioners, unjust, adulterers, or even as this publican. I fast twice in the week; I give tithes of all that I possess" (Luke 18:11-12).

The elder brother likewise boasted in imaginary righteousness when he complained about all the favors bestowed on his prodigal-but-repentant brother: "Lo, these many years do I serve thee; neither transgressed I at any time thy commandment; and yet thou never gavest me a kid, that I might make merry with my friends" (Luke 15:29).

Both the Pharisee and the pharisaic brother made the mistake of assuming they were in accord with divine righteousness, when in reality both were out of tune. How many today boast that by treating their neighbors right, attending church, and giving they earn acceptance before God, thereby glorying in their righteousness which in God's sight falls far short of the perfection He demands.

Christian people may be deceived as to the state of their

Christian progress. As one makes progress in holiness, he sees himself as being less holy. Approaching the whiteness of God's perfection causes one's own blemishes to stand out in dark contrast. This was the testimony of the Apostle Paul who, as he advanced in the Christian life, saw more clearly the depravity of his heart. In sequence, he claimed to be not one whit behind the apostles; then, least among the apostles; later, one not fit to be called a saint; and finally, the chief of sinners. As we grow in holiness we have a deeper sense of our sin. For a person to claim a great advance in holiness may indicate that his boasting is the outgrowth of self-deception.

Also, we may be spiritually deceived as to our state before God by imagining that because we once made a decision of consecration, we are automatically doing our best. The Christian life is a warfare, a constant struggle. We may be resting on past laurels when at that very moment we are surrounded by the enemy. We may think we are spiritually rich when really we are poor. Remember the condemnation of the Laodicean church: "Because thou sayest, I am rich, and increased with goods, and have need of nothing; and knowest not that thou are wretched, and miserable, and poor, and blind, and naked" (Rev. 3:17). We must be sure that we aren't boasting emptily in our testimonies.

Even in the giving of a testimony there is a tendency to boast of our part in salvation. It is as if we chose Christ rather than His choosing us. The Scripture says, "For by grace are ye saved through faith, and that not of yourselves. It is the gift of God; not of works, lest any man should boast" (Eph. 2:8-9).

David Brainerd wrote in his diary on April 1, 1742, "Where then is boasting? Surely it is excluded when we think how we are dependent on God for the being and every act of grace. Oh, if ever I get to heaven it will be because God wills, and nothing else; for I never did anything of myself but get away from God! My soul will be astonished at the unsearchable riches of divine grace when I arrive at the mansions, which the blessed Saviour is going before to prepare.''

Paul affirms that boasting should be excluded (Rom. 3:27). Jesus is both the Author and the Finisher of our faith.

Boasting of things not worthy of glory. Boasting of things known to be untrue is lying. Boasting of things not known to be untrue is self-deception. Boasting of things true but not worthy of glory is pride.

Aristotle, in his *Nicomachean Ethics,* has a paragraph on boasting. Among other things he wrote, "The boastful man then is thought to be apt to claim the things that bring glory, when he has not got them, or to claim more of them than he has.''

We boast because we overrate certain things and place too much hope, value, and dependence on them. These are false hopes, and glorying in them is wrong boasting.

Many glory in education, reason, and intellect. Rationalists place their hope of heaven and the salvation of the world on the superiority of reason and the ability of man to think his way out of his dilemmas. Philosophy and science are worshiped. Degrees are pursued. Education is good, but wisdom and learning cannot effect our salvation. The wisdom of this world is foolishness with God.

Giant Goliath boasted of his strength and made fun of the boy David. As Goliath strutted out, nine feet tall, clad in armor, and with implements of war, he vaunted his prowess and taunted his opponent; but he came to a humiliating end.

Punishment was pronounced on Assyria by God's prophet because Assyria had boasted of its conquests: "By the strength of my hand I have done it, and by my wisdom" (Isa. 10:13).

The King of Tyre was rebuked by Ezekiel because he said, "I am a God; I sit in the seat of God" (Ezek. 28:2).

Rab-shakeh, envoy from Assyria, boasted to citizens of Jerusalem of the power and might of his people (2 Kings 18:33-35).

There was also subtle boasting and open pride in Naaman's anger when the Prophet Elisha told him to dip seven times in the River Jordan: "Behold, I thought, he will surely come out to me, and stand, and call on the name of the Lord his God, and strike his hand over the place, and recover the leper" (2 Kings 5:11).

A classic example of a boaster who came to quick humiliation was Nebuchadnezzar. When Babylon was excavated, over a million bricks had Nebuchadnezzar's names and titles stamped on them. Once he boasted, "Is not this great Babylon, that I have built for the house of the kingdom by the might of my power, and for the honor of my majesty?" (Dan. 4:30) While these words were still in his mouth, he was told that the kingdom would depart from him and he would live like a beast among the grasses. He was to learn that it was God who gave him his power. The might, strength, and position of man is not equal to an infinitesimal fraction of God's power.

Some people boast about their incomes, bank balances, and investments. All could be snatched away in a few hours. These are poor items in which to glory.

Paul, before his conversion, boasted of his Hebrew ancestry. The Jews boasted that they had the Law and were chosen of God as Abraham's children. John the Baptist said that the Lord could raise up children to Himself from stones, as he urged them not to brag that they were Abraham's children. A rabbi once said, "He that hath his abode in Palestine is sure of eternal life."

We may claim descent from Calvin or Luther, Washington or Lincoln, or to be Episcopalians or Baptists for a dozen generations, but that does not count before God. We stand or fall on our own, not on the merits of our progenitors.

Subtle and various are the ways of boasting. Sometimes we boast by repeating a compliment given us by another. But Proverbs 27:1 says, "Let another man praise thee, and not thine own mouth."

Boasting of future plans. "Boast not thyself of tomorrow; for thou knowest not what a day may bring forth" (Prov. 27:1). Many put off salvation because they say there is lots of time. But some people who were laughing yesterday are silent in death today. We have no assurance of the future time allotted to us. To say, "I will think over the Gospel's claims later on" is presumption, for what guarantee does one have of the future?

How many people make plans for the future without taking God into account! Jesus related a parable of a foolish farmer who could not pack all his produce in his barn, so he built more storage space with the idea of taking it easy and being merry. But the farmer forgot that at any moment his soul might be required of him.

James gives some sound advice: "Go to now, ye that say, Today or tomorrow we will go into such a city, and continue there a year, and buy and sell, and get gain. Whereas ye know not what shall be on the morrow. For what is your life? It is even a vapor, that appeareth for a little time, and then vanisheth away. For that ye ought to say, If the Lord will, we shall live, and do this, or that. But now ye rejoice in your boastings; all such rejoicing is evil" (James 4:13-16).

Included in our proposed plans should be the spirit of, "If the Lord will" or, "The Lord willing." Otherwise we are boasting. How easy it is to make some vaunt as to future faithfulness to God, not realizing our weaknesses. Such was Peter's boast not to deny his Lord, and even a willingness to die. How much better to keep such boastings to ourselves and rather take heed lest, thinking we are well established, we miserably fall.

THE RIGHT KIND OF BOASTING

The text in Jeremiah (9:23-24) tells us where to glory—in the Lord and His goodness, judgment, and righteousness.

Here are some examples of proper boasting:

When Joseph was called out of the dungeon to interpret Pharaoh's dream, he said to Pharaoh, "It is not in me. God shall give Pharaoh an answer of peace" (Gen. 41:16). Joseph gave glory to God and refused to take any credit for himself.

Young David boasted of his exploits in killing a lion and a bear as he protected the sheep, but he gave honor to God by concluding, "The Lord that delivered me out of the paw of the lion, and out of the paw of the bear, He will deliver me out of the hand of this Philistine" (1 Sam. 17:37).

If boasting is to glorify self, it is wrong; but if the basic motive is to boast of God, it is proper boasting. "In God we boast all the day long, and praise Thy name forever" (Ps. 44:8). "My soul shall make her boast in the Lord" (Ps. 34:2).

When Paul boasted of his infirmities and sufferings, it was not for self-glory but for the advancement and glory of God (2 Cor. 12:1-11).

Man was made to honor God. When he honors any other thing or person, he is not achieving his end for, as the Westminster Confession of Faith says, "Man's chief end is to glorify God and enjoy Him forever." So boasting in the Lord will help us fulfill our true natures as members of the human race.

Former champion mile-runner Gil Dodds, in giving a word to the public over the microphone after a race, never made a practice of saying, "Look at my speed. Can't I run?" but, "I thank God who helped me. I can do all things through Christ which strengtheneth me."

A little over a century ago a famous man lived who was an outstanding portrait painter, artist, and sculptor. He also wrote hundreds of published articles. For years he was a college professor. He was also known as the father of American photography. Among other things, he invented the telegraph. His name was Samuel F.B. Morse. When Morse was an old man, the telegraphers of the United States and Canada chipped in and had a statue made in his honor. They unveiled the statue, and over 2,000 of them gathered to watch for Morse's message of thanks to come over the wires. Morse sent this message, "Glory to God in the highest. On earth peace, good will toward men." The telegraphers cheered wildly. Morse could have shouted, "Look what I did!" The whole world was honoring his feats. But in the hour of victory he could only repeat these words over and over again: "Bless the Lord, O my soul, and forget not all His benefits."

The usual items in which people boast—wisdom, riches, might—are temporary and can flit away without a moment's notice. But our Lord is eternal and those linked to Him and His purposes can glory in Him and His salvation, for these are eternal. With Paul may we say, "God forbid that I should glory, save in the cross of our Lord Jesus Christ, by whom the world is crucified unto me, and I unto the world" (Gal. 6:14).

As we contemplate Christ's laying aside of glory, when He could have stayed in heaven and kept His glory, how melted and humble our hearts must become. He who was equal with God made Himself of no reputation. He who was somebody became nobody. Let us follow in His steps. And may our boasting be in Him.

> When I survey the wondrous cross,
>   On which the Prince of glory died,
> My richest gain I count but loss,
>   And pour contempt on all my pride.
>
> Forbid it, Lord, that I should boast,
>   Save in the death of Christ my God;
> All the vain things that charm me most,
>   I sacrifice them to His blood.

TEN
SONGS AT MIDNIGHT

Two women were driving home from a concert in which a violinist had given a virtually perfect performance. "Wasn't it wonderful?" one exclaimed.

"I didn't like it at all," the other retorted. "The way he blew his nose after that first number ruined the evening for me."

Some folks complain habitually, missing the music and hearing only the blowing of the nose. A cartoon showed a man asking an older friend, "Well, Brother Jones, I hear you are retiring. Have you made any retirement plans?"

Came Brother Jones' answer, "Yep, I plan to complain a lot." Though some people are born with a heart murmur, far more develop a murmuring tongue.

"The Grumbler Song" goes like this:

In country, town, or city, some people can be found
Who spend their lives in grumbling at everything around;

O yes, they always grumble, no matter what we say,
For these are chronic grumblers and they grumble night and day.

Chorus:
O they grumble on Monday, Tuesday, Wednesday,
Grumble on Thursday too,
Grumble on Friday, Saturday, Sunday,
Grumble the whole week through.

They grumble in the city, they grumble on the farm;
They grumble at their neighbors, they think it is no harm;
They grumble at their husbands, they grumble at their wives;
They grumble at their children, but the grumbler never thrives.

They grumble when it's raining, they grumble when it's dry;
And if the crops are failing, they grumble and they sigh.
They grumble at low prices and grumble when they're high;
They grumble all the year around and they grumble till they die.
—Anonymous

Those who use the tongue to complain, murmur, and grumble disobey God's Word. Paul wrote, "Do all things without murmurings" (Phil. 2:14).

THE FACTS OF THE GRUMBLING TONGUE
Some people, born pessimists, always see the dark side of things rather than the bright. An optimist may be wrong as often as a pessimist, but he is far happier. Two men looked up. One saw a beautiful silver lining of a cloud; the other saw the cloud's black center. Two boys were gathering grapes. One was happy because he gathered so many grapes; the other moaned because the grapes contained seeds. Two girls saw a bright-green bush. One

was thrilled with its beautiful roses; the other complained because it had thorns. Two men conversed on a rainy day. One commented how wonderful it was that the parched ground was getting rain; the other growled about the weather.

> Two men look out through the same bars;
> One sees mud, and one the stars.
> —Author unknown

The Israelites were chronic murmurers. Their history from even before their deliverance from Egypt to their entrance into the Promised Land buzzes with an undertone of murmur. In fact, the Book of Numbers, which contains the record of their wilderness wanderings, could be called "the book of murmurings." The early chapters of Exodus also report some of their complaints.

When their daily task was increased during the days of their bondage, the Israelites murmured. On the first leg of the Exodus, pursued by Pharaoh, they groaned, "Because there were no graves in Egypt, hast thou taken us away to die in the wilderness?" (Ex. 14:11)

After the miraculous parting of the Red Sea and their marvelous deliverance, the Israelites sang. A naive observer might have thought that never again would one word of discontent pass their lips. But before long they registered another murmur because they had no drinking water, for the waters of Marah were bitter: "What shall we drink?" (15:24)

When they had no food, they grumbled again. "Would to God we had died by the hand of the Lord in the land of Egypt, when we sat by the flesh pots, and when we did eat bread to the full; for ye have brought us forth into this wilderness, to kill this whole assembly with hunger" (16:3). Manna was the result of this murmuring.

Later at Rephidim the people again thirsted for water. Forget-

ting that God had given them water before in time of need, they
murmured against Moses: "Wherefore is this that thou hast
brought us up out of Egypt, to kill us and our children and our
cattle with thirst?" (17:3)

THE WRONGNESS OF GRUMBLING
The Lord, who heard the complaints of the Israelites, hears all
murmurings. Murmurings against God's servants are grumblings
against God. When criticisms were made against the nation's
leaders, Moses warned, "Your murmurings are not against us,
but against the Lord" (16:8).

*Not only is God disturbed by our grumbling, but sometimes it
confuses others.* The head of a family used to ask the blessing
every morning before breakfast. One morning, immediately after
thanking God for the food, he began to grumble about hard
times, the poor quality of food, the way it was cooked, and much
more. His little daughter interrupted, "Daddy, do you suppose
God heard what you prayed a little while ago?"

"Certainly," he replied, thinking that he was giving his
daughter a lesson in prayer.

"And did He hear what you said about the bacon and the
coffee?"

The father's reply, "Of course," was not so confident.

"Then, Daddy, which does God believe?"

Among the reasons given for God's displeasure with the
wandering Israelites, along with idolatry and fornication, was
murmuring. "Neither murmur ye, as some of them also murmured, and were destroyed of the destroyer" (1 Cor. 10:10).

When the people complained, the Lord's anger was kindled
and a fire consumed many. The Lord said He would send
pestilences among them so that only two, Joshua and Caleb,
would ever reach the Promised Land. In fact, the people's

number of years of wandering was directly proportional to the number of days the spies searched out the land. But the two who gave a minority report of faith, rather than of complaint, reached the Promised Land.

When Korah opposed Moses, the ground opened up to consume him and his followers. Murmuring also caused God to send fiery serpents among the Israelites.

Grumbling reveals a lot about us. Grumbling is serious not only because God hates it, but because it reflects what lurks in the hidden recesses of our hearts. Murmuring is a secret, furtive thing. The Israelites murmured in their tents (Deut. 1:27). Pastor David Smith of Eden Chapel, Cambridge, England wrote in *The Evangelical Magazine of Wales,* "Murmuring is an evil that rarely sees the light of day. Sometimes when digging a piece of land the garden fork will overturn a large stone. And there, unexpectedly exposed to the light, are a dozen little creatures scurrying for the darkness in which their lives are spent. Such a creature is the murmurer."

Murmuring has an undesirable effect on the murmurer. Winston Churchill used to tell the story of a family that went on a picnic. Suddenly during the afternoon a five-year-old fell into the lake. None of the adults could swim. Everyone panicked. At great risk a passerby dove in fully clothed, managed to rescue the sinking child, and presented him safe and sound to his mother.

Instead of thanking the stranger for his brave act, the mother snapped complainingly at the hero, "Where's Johnny's cap?" Not surprisingly in all the commotion the boy's cap had been displaced. Out of all the aspects of the episode, the woman found something with which to be dissatisfied.

A proverb rightly says that discontent "makes men's lips like rusty hinges, seldom to move without murmuring and complaining."

Murmuring is not only bad itself, but it constantly lives with bad company. Here are some of its bedfellows:

Unbelief in God. Murmuring often springs from lack of trust in God. Most of the Israelitish grumbling was primed from the pump of unbelief. When the Egyptians pursued, they forgot that God could deliver them, and so complained. God opened the Red Sea and provided escape. Shortly afterward they longed for Egypt, for they had no food or water. Could not He who parted the waters of the Red Sea provide water and manna? He did. Later they again complained because of no water. They forgot God's previous manifestation of power.

Centuries later Elijah sat down under a juniper tree and begged to die. "It is enough; now, O Lord, take away my life" (1 Kings 19:4). The Lord told him there were 7,000 who had not bowed the knee to Baal. Elijah thought he was the only true-blue servant of God left. Such a self-pity contradicts a radiant hopefulness and trust in God.

Christians sometimes groan against the will of God. Tragedy or affliction comes our way and we blame God. Some have stopped going to church because God hasn't been good to them. How dangerous, for they really say, "God, You don't know what is best for me. I know more than You, God."

Ingratitude. Discontented speech often overlooks blessings. Ingratitude is a real sin. It says, "I forget the many things for which I should be thankful." Murmuring stems from a short memory which forgets to count blessings.

Murmuring may lead to the injury of others. "Thou shalt not covet," the last of the Ten Commandments, may sound harmless and even undeserving of a place in the Decalogue. But covetousness is a pivotal matter for it leads to the breaking of other commandments. Coveting another's wife may lead to adultery and murder. Coveting another's property may lead to stealing. Coveting another's reputation may lead to false witness. Murmuring is linked to discontent which leads to covetousness, and in turn, to overt iniquity.

King Ahab pouted over Naboth's vineyard. Lurking covetousness led to the false accusation and liquidation of Naboth.

Saul uttered words of discontent when the women praised David more than him. Later Saul sought David's life.

The disciples, murmuring among themselves as to who should be greatest, revealed an inordinate desire for prominence, which led to repeated arguments on the same subject, one of them shamefully in the Upper Room on the night before Jesus died.

A man complained to Jesus, "Master, speak to my brother, that he divide the inheritance with me." Jesus answered, "Beware of covetousness" (Luke 12:13-15). Jesus knew that such murmuring could lead to family feuding.

When Mary anointed Jesus with perfume that cost the equivalent of a year's salary, Judas objected, because he wanted the ointment sold so that he might steal the proceeds. His murmuring was just a cover for his thievery.

People of Jericho murmured when they saw Jesus going to eat at the home of Zaccheus, a chief tax collector who had likely become rich through dishonest transactions. Their complaining attitude would have excluded Zaccheus, the very kind of sinner-person Jesus had come to seek and to save.

The murmuring of Grecians against the Hebrews, because their widows were neglected in the daily ministration, could have precipitated a serious rift in the early Jesusalem church. But it was prevented by the wise suggestion of the apostles to choose seven godly and gifted men to oversee the distribution of daily necessities (Acts 6:1-3).

Sometimes a person who speaks openly has a more difficult time securing a hearing than a whisperer. Because many seem ready to listen to gossip, murmuring can act like leaven, quietly spreading resentment and discord among the brethren.

A Springfield, Illinois neighbor was drawn to his door one day by the sound of crying children. He saw Abraham Lincoln passing by with his two sons who were whimpering. "What's the matter with the boys?" asked the solicitous neighbor.

"Just what's the matter with the whole world," answered Lincoln. "I have three walnuts, and each boy wants two."

Much of our domestic, economic, and international dissension springs from a grumbling spirit.

HOW TO OVERCOME
THE GRUMBLING TONGUE

A secular magazine ran an article, "How to Complain." Here are some of its suggestions: Nastiness gets you nowhere, so begin with a compliment. Then appeal, "I have a problem and I need your help." Don't demand. Anger and sarcasm make your opponent defensive. Present your complaint face to face, if possible. If you have to write, remember that vitriolic letters are counterproductive. Prepare a clear, logical, case with copies of corroborating documents (*New York,* January 7, 1985).

These suggestions most likely apply to legitimate complaints. Here are some helps in overcoming the bad habit of chronic griping.

Contentment. Paul had suffered deeply, and had been shipwrecked, stoned, beaten, and buffeted. Yet he said, "I have learned in whatsoever state I am, therewith to be content" (Phil. 4:11).

Often people with much of this world's goods toss constantly on the sea of discontent, while others who have few material possessions radiate a cheerful peace. If we would each introspectively examine his own status, we would find that we have much to make us content.

A man, dissatisfied with his small estate, wanted a better one. So he hired an agent to write an advertisement describing the estate. When the ad was ready, the agent took it to the gentleman and read the description of the estate to him. "Read that again," asked the owner. The agent again read the ad. "I don't think I'll sell after all," said the man. "I've been looking for an estate like that all my life, and I didn't know I owned it."

A little meditation will reveal to most discontented people that their lot in life is not so bad after all. An essay tells how Jupiter issued a proclamation that all people could bring their troubles to one place and drop them in a common heap. Many people brought all kinds of miseries—diseases, poverty, worries; one man brought his wife. When the pile was finished, Jupiter gave a second order. Each one should now choose some affliction in place of his own. Each person reluctantly began to choose a trouble other than the one he had brought; but before long a sorry howl went up from the people, now unhappier than ever. They so filled the air with their grumbling that Jupiter in pity gave them permission to take back their original burdens. Simultaneously, he sent a goddess named Patience to teach all the people how to bear their miseries in the easiest manner. Then the people dispersed happily.

Two grasshoppers jumped into a pail of milk. One groaned, moaned, and finally sank to the bottom. The other remained cheerful, kicking his legs, churning until the milk became butter. That grasshopper then walked over the top and jumped away. If we cultivate a contented attitude in our troubles, they will become stepping-stones to happiness.

Thankfulness. For every vexation we may have there is a goodness to counteract it. Our troubles are outnumbered in quantity and outvalued in quality by our blessings.

A Swedish proverb says, "Those who wish to sing always find a song." We always can find something to be thankful for; so let us magnify our blessings and minimize our troubles. A Welsh miner was converted during the great Welsh revival. His fellow workers thought they would vex him to see how he would behave; so they stole his dinner pail. Expecting his usual angry oath, they were surprised when he smiled and said, "Praise the Lord! I've still got my appetite. They can't take that!"

Trust in God. If God delivered us once, can't He keep on watching over us? Doesn't He know what is best for our lives? Examples in Scripture of those who triumphed over difficulties without murmuring were given to encourage us to learn trust in the Sovereign of the universe, who does all things well.

Job exercised masterful acquiesence after tragedy came. Though his children, possessions, and health were gone, he said, "The Lord gave, and the Lord hath taken away; blessed be the name of the Lord. In all this Job sinned not, nor charged God foolishly" (Job 1:21-22).

Peter and the other apostles were whipped by the Sanhedrin merely for preaching the Gospel. Most of us would whimper and whine, "Lord, what's the use of serving You? I'm quitting, for when I witness for You, I get whipped." But they departed from the presence of the council, rejoicing that they were counted worthy to suffer shame for His name.

Paul and Silas were thrown into the Philippian jail for casting a demon out of a maiden. We probably would complain, "Lord, look at what happens when we serve You. We're through." But they sang praises at midnight!

A supreme example of contentment under trial was our Saviour. A pastor of a small-town church, very unhappy because of his trials, became an inveterate grumbler. He constantly found fault with his members because he imagined they mistreated him. A brother minister came to hold special services. True to form, the pastor at the close of the first Sunday morning service began to pour out his doleful story. "You've no idea of my troubles. The way my members treat me is unspeakable."

The visiting minister propounded the following questions:

"Did they ever spit in your face? Did they ever smite you?"

"Why, no!"

"Did they ever crown you with thorns?"

This last question forced the pastor to bow his head. The other continued, "Your Master and mine was treated like that. All His followers forsook Him and fled, leaving Him in the hands of wicked men. Yet He opened not His mouth."

The effect of the conversation was amazing. Both ministers bowed in prayer. The discouraged pastor became a happy man.

A recent testimony bears out the truth that praise rather than complaint may be ours in the hour of deep affliction. On October 12, 1984 Dr. James Cummings, former missionary to the Philippines and member of the faculty of Denver Conservative Baptist Seminary, spoke these stirring words in the school's chapel service:

"In an earlier day Dizzy Dean, the famous baseball pitcher, was hit on the head. People were concerned about what had happened, and in the paper the next day the headlines read, 'X ray of Dean's head shows nothing.' "

"I wish that today I could say that to you about the X rays and tests that have been taken of me in recent days. My doctor's report was a rather serious and grave one as he told me that I have one of the most powerful kinds of cancer that people get. It races through the bloodstream like an Olympic Gold Medalist gobbling up all the good tissue it can find along the way.

"As I received that report I was filled with many emotions, even while realizing that our lives are in God's hands. Just as there are seasons around us in this world of nature and beauty, there are also birth and death. And there are seasons of Spring, Summer, Fall, and Winter. We are reminded of this even now as the days are growing shorter and the leaves are falling. So I ask of you that you would remember me and my family at this special time. You will perhaps see the leaves falling from these branches and this trunk, but I do not ask that you feel sorry for me.

"At a similar time, Hubert Humphrey, suffering through a bout with cancer, said these words: 'The greatest gift that has come to me is the affection of so many people. Far more important than people feeling sorry tor me—in fact, feeling sorry for someone is simply to give him a little pain reliever—is the love that is a healing force.·

"I thank you for your love and your prayers, and I would just like to close with the reading of this rich and powerful passage of the love of God from Romans, chapter eight (NIV):

> Who will bring any charge against those whom God has chosen? It is God who justifies. Who is he that condemns? Christ Jesus, who died—more than that, who was raised to life—is at the right hand of God and is also interceding for us. Who shall separate us from the love of Christ? Shall trouble or hardship or persecution or famine or nakedness or danger or sword? As it is written: "For Your sake we face death all day long; we are considered as sheep to be slaughtered." No, in all these things we are more than conquerors through Him who loved us. For I am convinced that neither death nor life, neither angels nor demons, neither the present nor the future, nor any powers, neither height nor depth, nor anything else in all creation, will be able to separate us from the love of God that is in Christ Jesus our Lord.

The hymn-writer says,

> Lord, I would clasp Thy hand in mine,
> Nor ever murmur nor repine,
> Content, whatever lot I see,
> Since 'tis Thy hand that leadeth me!

ELEVEN

THERMOMETER AND THERMOSTAT

In a recently released film on the life of George Beverly Shea, *Then Sings My Soul*, a humorous moment results from his sister's observation that, "Mother never says anything bad about anyone. I'm going to catch her at the supper table tonight."

At the meal, Shea's sister asked, "Mother, what do you think of the devil?" She thought she had her mother cornered.

Her mother paused, then replied, "I admire his persistence."

Her gentle reply reflected their mother's disposition. But in addition to revealing the state of our Christian maturity, the tongue can also govern our conduct. Like that device on our wall, which both records and regulates temperature, our tongue serves both as a thermometer and a thermostat.

Two strong assertions in the Book of James point to these

roles. The first relates to the thermometer's function, stating that the measure in which a person governs his tongue is an index of his whole moral nature. "For we all make many mistakes, and if anyone makes no mistakes in what he says he is a perfect man, able to bridle the whole body also" (James 3:2, RSV).

The second thought, an advance on the first, deals with the thermostat's function, claiming that the tongue is a controlling instrument, not just indicating direction but determining it. "If we put bits into the mouth of horses that they may obey us, we guide their whole bodies. Look at the ships also; though they are so great and are driven by strong winds, they are guided by a very small rudder wherever the will of the pilot directs" (James 3:3-4, RSV).

AS THERMOMETER

A man remembers how each spring his mother used to say, "Son, put out your tongue and let me see what it's like." Then after a quick look she would say, "Oh no, you're not in good condition," and then make him take some horrible concoction. The Great Physician can tell our spiritual status by an examination of our tongues. He Himself said, "By thy words thou shalt be justified, and by thy words thou shalt be condemned" (Matt. 12:37).

Just as a gauge on the dashboard of a car indicates the amount of gas in the tank, so our conversation reveals the level of our spiritual vitality. No offense in speech marks a perfect person; some offense, a moderately imperfect person; much offense, a deeply imperfect person. Examination of anyone's speech will prove that person is still imperfect. The only perfect One was the God-Man, Jesus Christ, in whose mouth was found no guile, who when reviled reviled not again, whose lips were full of grace, and of whom it was said, "Never man spake like this

Man'' (John 7:46). Perfection of speech could never be attrib-
uted to Moses, John, Peter, Paul, or any other mere human.

A lady told her preacher that she liked him except for one
thing. She asked if she could take her scissors and shorten his tie.
He kindly agreed, and when she was through, he asked a like
privilege. When she reluctantly agreed, he replied, ''Put out
your tongue!''

Perhaps more often you have felt like cutting off your own
tongue and have even started the process by biting it! In the
proportion that one's tongue needs shortening, his spiritual life
falls short.

Why is one's tongue an accurate index of his advance in
holiness?

Mastery indicative of much grace. An old farmer used to
remark that the hardest thing to catch and tether is not a pig, a
sheep, or a lively heifer but the human tongue; and nothing is so
much in need of being tied down. Someone suggested it is the
last hurdle in the Christian race, which when overcome means
we have virtually arrived. If a person can bridle his tongue, he
proves he can bridle all else.

The main reason for difficulty in governing the tongue is its
wide scope for doing wrong. Speech can be violated so frequently and in so many ways. Some temptations provide oppor-
tunities for their enticements only occasionally and under limited
circumstances, such as murder, thievery, and adultery. But to sin
with words is a constant temptation, for we are using words
almost incessantly. And they can erupt so easily into many
aberrations, such as lying, criticizing, and complaining.

A young man who lived in a boardinghouse was studying
shorthand. He decided to practice in the evenings by taking
down every word spoken in the living room as the men chatted.
''Years later,'' said the man, ''I went over my notebooks and
found that in four months of incessant conversation, no one had

said anything that made any difference to anybody.''

Centuries ago men used to gather where three roads came together south of ancient Rome and talk of things. The Latin for three roads is *tria via,* from which we get our English "trivia." Conversation can easily degenerate into idle words.

If a military commander could surround and hem in a city which has a thousand outlets, he could certainly lay successful siege to a city with fewer exits. A man who can command his tongue, which can run wild in so many ways, certainly can control other avenues of temptation.

Inflexibility here indicative of lack of compromise elsewhere. The natural tendency is to think lightly of hasty expressions vented in moments of excitement, slight misrepresentations, impure innuendoes, profane jokes, and sly insinuations. However, the Lord will not hold him guiltless who hurls words around in a careless fashion. He who would please the Lord must take a serious view of this matter.

He who thinks gravely of wrong words likely will take a solemn view of wrong deeds. A person's care for proper speech betokens similar care for proper conduct.

Answering a phone call, a little girl said, "My big sis is at evening school, taking a course in domestic silence," which might not be a bad choice for all of us to enroll in.

Reflection of that which lies in the heart. Just as Peter's accent gave him away, so what we say exposes the workings of our hearts. Swearwords disclose profane hearts; impure stories emanate from filthy hearts; murmurings come from thankless hearts; criticisms unveil jealous hearts.

Thus a more excellent indicator of a person's spirituality is not abstinence from certain practices but tongue control. Modern pharisaism, which has reduced godliness to abstinence from certain questionable pleasures, forgets that the Bible does not mention these directly, whereas it unequivocally condemns bitterness, anger, evil-speaking, backbiting, and censoriousness. One pastor stated that he would rather have his parishioners in a place of worldly amusement on prayer meeting night than loitering around after the midweek meeting assassinating someone's reputation. When a woman spoke to her pastor about some other woman in the congregation who used too much makeup, the pastor replied, "It is less evil for a woman to redden her cheeks than for another to blacken her character."

The right use of one's tongue evinces spiritual maturity. The moral power of a man who can govern his tongue is unlimited.

AS THERMOSTAT
The hands of a watch announce the time but in no way alter it. A thermometer registers temperature but in no way regulates it. But a thermostat does govern temperature. Similarly, a tongue not only measures moral progress but is a determining instrument.

The tongue is spoken of under the figures of bit and rudder. A bit determines the course of a horse, making him turn to the left or right, letting him run fast or jolting him to slow his progress. Just so a rudder guides a ship's course, turning it in any desired direction. Proper use of the tongue can steer a person safely through dangerous roads or rocks.

As a thermostat, the tongue can lower the temperatures of temper, pride, jealousy, spite, and other sins of the spirit and make us more like the Lord Jesus Christ. In the Book of James we read, "Let every man be swift to hear, slow to speak, slow to wrath" (1:19).

Swift to hear. Everyday practice often reverses James' advice, making it, "Be swift to speak, slow to hear." However, the biblical order agrees with our biological construction, for we are so built that listening is easier than talking. We have two ears and only one tongue. The ears are exposed, enabling them to do their work more easily. The tongue is walled in by the teeth and mouth. Furthermore, ears are not made to shut; the mouth is so constructed so it permits constant closing.

The wisdom of the swift ear and the slow tongue has been expressed in countless maxims: "Man has two ears and only one mouth; he should be more ready to hear than speak." "Speech is silver; silence is golden." "Better remain silent and be thought a fool than speak and remove all doubt." "Think twice before you speak once."

One wise man said, "Experience has taught me that whenever anything is on the tip of my tongue I should keep it there." Another quipped, "Look before you lip." Still another remarked, "A good listener is not only popular everywhere but after a while he knows something." A Scottish proverb says, "Keep your tongue a prisoner and your body will go free."

Though swiftness to hear is good advice in general, it was a particular kind of listener James had in mind. Instruction in the early church was chiefly oral. Books were scarce, many of the New Testament epistles had not been written when James wrote his letter, and the mass communication media of press, radio, movies, and television did not exist. For most people the ear was the main avenue of learning. Hence Christians were to attend the meeting place of the church regularly and to listen again and again to the divine message.

But not all listened. Some talkative, contentious folks liked to interrupt, speak up, discuss, and question. The motive in many cases was delight at hearing one's voice, love of controversy, or vanity of displaying knowledge. The resultant needless debate profited neither the speaker nor the listener. James doubtless had been present in assemblies on such occasions and wrote from firsthand observation. Thus came the command, "Be swift to hear," which applies not only to religious discussions but to all conversation.

The Lord has not lodged the fullness of His gifts in any one person. Since wisdom and ability are fragmentary in any one individual, each has information his neighbor lacks. This diversity of knowledge makes us mutually interdependent, so that a mechanic can learn from a philosopher and a philosopher from a mechanic. All of us should cultivate the disposition of humility in the presence of others, plus the desire to extract from their conversations some bits of information. Since all knowledge will not die with any one person, no one should monopolize a conversation.

Edward Hersey Richards has written,

> A wise old owl lived in an oak;
> The more he saw the less he spoke;
> The less he spoke the more he heard:
> Why can't we all be like that bird?*

A young man went to Socrates to learn oratory. When introduced to the philosopher, he talked so incessantly that Socrates asked for a double fee. "Why charge me double?" asked the young fellow.

"Because," said the philosopher, "I must teach you two sciences. The one, how to hold your tongue, and the other, how to speak. The first science is more difficult!"

In order to let our tongues function as thermostats, we must first learn readiness to listen.

Slow to speak. Parallel with swiftness of ear is slowness of speech. A tourist spending the night in a small Vermont town joined a group of men sitting on the porch of the general store. After several unsuccessful efforts to start conversation, he finally

---

*A Treasury of the Familiar, ed. Ralph L. Woods (New York: The Macmillan Co., 1952), p. 96. Used by permission of The Macmillian Co.

asked, "Is there a law against talking in this town?"

"No law against it," drawled one Vermonter, "but there's an understanding that no one's to speak unless he's positive he can improve on the silence."

A danger of profuse talking is that one must talk about something. In the multitude of words we may mention another's secret or faults, which might have gone unsaid. Verbosity increases the mathematical probability of talebearing, character dissection, argumentation, and self-glory.

James does not forbid the brethren to speak in church meetings but urges them to be slow to speak. His thought could be paraphrased: "When discussion of religious subjects crops up either in worship assemblies or in private groups, above all, seek to enlighten your minds and warm your hearts. Listen humbly to what the others have to say. Should you participate—and this is permissible, for genuine questions and honest doubts have their place—speak in a spirit of love, keep rancor out of your voice, and do not try to show off your knowledge, but rather interject your remarks with the desire to discover the truth for the spiritual profit of all present. Be swift to hear, slow to speak."

Slow to wrath. But the brethren were not restraining their tongues in the assemblies. Perhaps this practice carried over from servics in synagogues, which were sometimes noisy places. The synagogue service at Nazareth ended in an uproar the day Jesus came back to His hometown to preach, with the wrathful people trying to push Him over a cliff. Paul usually met with contradiction and blasphemy in the synagogues.

With the tendency to talk transported into early church meetings, some delighted to put themselves forward in debate. Others would refute. Much heat was generated—more heat than light. Thermostat tongues turned the heat up. Some persons turned on each other in fierce controversy and wild denunciation, calling names, even to the point of cursing. This is suggested by James' accusation, "Therewith [by the tongue] bless we God, even the Father; and therewith curse we men. . . . Out of the same mouth proceedeth blessing and cursing" (James 3:9-10).

The thermostat tongue which can turn the heat up can also turn it down, if used rightly. Here is a man with a strong temper, exceedingly irritable, who bursts forth frequently, making everyone around him miserable. He cannot control his feelings within, for they are like a fretful horse that is too much for its rider, or like fiercely driven ships, swaying in one direction, then the other.

But even though this man cannot control his feelings, can he not, if he pleases, refrain from speaking or else speak softly, avoiding needling, insulting replies? If through God's help he keeps his resolve not to say a single irritating word, the whole feeling within him will subside. Like the thermostat, the tongue can control inner heat. A soft answer turns away our own wrath as well as the anger of others.

But how easily the tongue adds fuel to the fire. How often people say, "When I speak on that subject, I get angry!" James calls the tongue incendiary, a little fire which kindles a great matter. One researcher looked into the reason why a scold, a woman with a wagging tongue, was dunked in water for punishment. He came to the conclusion that dunking had reference to putting out the fire of one's tongue, as mentioned by James. Tongue control can keep inflammatory thoughts from reaching the level of speech.

A person who takes care to consider what he says, and is thus slow to speak, will also be slow to wrath. The boiling passion within will slowly abate, if the tongue remains silent or speaks conciliatorily. Counting slowly to 10 before speaking gives the anger time to ebb away, cooling the flame.

The tongue can control jealousy and criticism. Envy often leads to tearing down another in the same line of work. One employee insinuates of a more successful worker, "Oh, he got ahead because he knows someone higher up in the organization." A soldier who received a promotion, home on furlough for two weeks before going overseas, wore his military clothes every day. A neighbor whose son received no advancement said, "Why doesn't Bob wear his civvies instead of showing off that he's an officer?" The truth was that Bob had lost 60 pounds in the service so his civilian clothes didn't fit, and he did not wish to buy new clothes just before embarking overseas.

Often we conquer our critical thoughts most effectively by absolutely refusing to allow them to be expressed in words. Bonhoeffer termed this "the ministry of holding one's tongue." He advocated as a decisive rule of Christian fellowships that every believer refrain from saying much that occurs to him. The practice of this discipline will amazingly enable an individual to cease from constantly evaluating, examining, and condemning the other person.

In their book, *Long-Term Marriage*, Floyd and Harriett Thatcher point out how "the use of right words can creatively avert hostility and misunderstanding in moments of crisis. For example, during the 1962 Cuban crisis when Russia and the United States confronted each other because of the presence of missiles in Cuba, the world hovered breathlessly for several days on the verge of a possible nuclear disaster. Instead of a blockade, President Kennedy imposed a *quarantine* on Cuba. A blockade would have been an act of war, but nobody knew just what the implications were to a *quarantine*. At the same time, the use of that word gave a clear signal that we intended to protect ourselves, but also indicated that we wanted, if at all possible, to avoid war. Consequently, the use of the word *quarantine*, intentionally vague, was part of our strategy. It was this careful and thoughtful choice of a word which helped forestall shooting until tempers cooled and reason could prevail" (*Word Books*, 1980, pp. 77-78). U.S. leaders cooled their own anger as well as those of the Russians by judicial use of the tongue.

Likewise, the tongue can serve as a thermostat to tone down pride. The haughty horse of arrogance will ride wildly if given half a chance. How quickly we interject words of self-congratulation, boasting, or running ourselves down with mock modesty, hoping that others will contradict our self-humbling statements, praise us, and cater to our pride. A safe rule orders that we obtrude self as little as possible into conversations with others. Refraining from all talking about oneself will restrain many a spark which easily could ignite into explosive pride.

Similarly, the tongue can control an inordinate desire for popularity. The wish to be a hail and hearty fellow well-met drives many to utter questionable jests, sarcasm, or gossip. The horse of popularity can ride roughshod unless controlled by the tongue.

The tongue can control profanity. The punctuation of conversation with an oath can easily get out of hand and end in much swearing. A pause to think before swearing can break the profane attitude and assist toward simple speech.

The tongue can control murmuring. When the weather is hot, we feel it more if we complain about it more. When we have a complaint, its frequent mention only agitates the trouble and makes us grumble all the more. Refusal to speak of our miseries can lower the feeling of discontent.

The tongue can control stress. Don't we all talk aloud to ourselves on occasion, such as when learning a new skill such as driving a car? In the privacy of your car you give yourself instructions. "Put the key in ignition. Turn key. Pump gas pedal. Look behind before backing up." Talking to yourself helps you get through a new stressful pattern of behavior till it becomes automatic. Similarly when times of stress and distress come our way, instead of letting our souls moan to us, "Everything's against me," we should speak to our souls, as did King David of old when threatened with discouragement: "Why art thou cast down, O my soul? And why art thou disquieted in me? Hope thou in God; for I shall yet praise Him for the help of His countenance" (Ps. 42:5). On one occasion "David was greatly distressed, for the people spake of stoning him . . . but David encouraged himself in the Lord his God" (1 Sam. 30:6). In times of trouble we can talk to ourselves, even out loud, about the greatness, goodness, and sovereignty of God. And the reminder that all things work together for good for God's children (Rom. 8:28) can also help allay distress.

Inside us are thoughts. When these boil up, they affect our words and our deeds. Our words stand midway between our thoughts and deeds. It is true that our words indicate what we are thinking. But it is also true that before these kindling thoughts erupt into a devastating fire, the proper use of a thermostat tongue can extinguish the threatening flames.

Some years ago Vice-President Agnew's mouth was covered by an address label on the cover of all copies of *Time* magazine printed at its Atlanta plant. The production error was caused by an out-of-adjustment machine that normally affixes the label in the lower left-hand corner. Similar maladjustments were found in labeling machines at other plants and corrected before mailing. How often many of us wish our mouths had been covered by a label or something, instead of blurting out some injudicious remark.

During a dinner in a large English home, at which a number of churchmen were guests, a woman was very busy with her tongue. She turned to a noted church worker who had been silent throughout the discussion, and asked, "In view of our argument, what do you hold?"

The response was, "My tongue!"

TWELVE

BETTER SWEET THAN BITTERSWEET

The late Senator Everett Dirksen, of Illinois, wishing to select a good birthday present for his wife, picked out a clever parrot and had it delivered. When he arrived home for dinner, he asked if the present had arrived.

"Oh yes," his wife replied, "it's in the oven. It'll be ready soon."

Shocked and chagrined, the Senator asked, "Why did you do that? I paid $75 for that parrot! It was such a smart bird!"

His wife replied, "If it was such a smart bird, why didn't it speak up?"

The tongue is meant to speak up. But when it does, it strangely and sadly spews out both good and bad words.

It was said of an exemplary colonial woman that she was dutiful, prudent, and diligent and that she placed a strong and constant guard on the door of her lips. No one ever heard her call an ill name, or detract from anybody (Carl Holliday, *Woman's Life in Colonial Days*, p. 130).

141

On the other hand, too many of us let our tongues run off with our brains. We talk too much, explain too much, and reveal too much to too many. Too often we have to talk ourselves out of bad situations because we didn't keep our mouths shut in the first place. In the Jewish Press, Morris Mandel writes, "Gossip is the most deadly microbe. It has neither legs nor wings. It is composed entirely of tales, and most of them have stings."

The tongue possesses the potential for both good and evil. Proverbs says, "Death and life are in the power of the tongue" (Prov. 18:21).

James points out this Jekyll-and-Hyde characteristic of the tongue. How incongruous for the same tongue to bless God and blister men. "Therewith bless we God, even the Father; and therewith curse we men, which are made after the similitude of God. Out of the same mouth proceedeth blessing and cursing" (James 3:9-10). This practice is as contradictory as bowing before a king, then throwing mud at his royal portrait.

At one moment the early Christian assembly praised God; then they preyed on their fellowmen. James then points out that the simplest objects rebuke such inconsistency: "Doth a fountain send forth at the same place sweet water and bitter? Can the fig tree, my brethren, bear olive berries? Either a vine, figs? So can no fountain both yield saltwater and fresh" (3:11-12).

The absurdity of going to a drinking tap and getting a glass of fresh, cold water and a minute later getting another glass which yields a bitter taste! The incredibility of fig trees bearing olive berries! It's just as incompatible for a mouth to spurt praise, then seconds later spew poison. Bittersweet may be the name of a palatable chocolate, but their combination in the realms of drinking water, fruit, and conversation is most unsavory.

The *New York Times*, editorializing on a famous general, called this colorful personality both "deeply religious and violently profane." Man may call such a blend colorful, but the

Bible condemns it as a sinful anomaly. Yet the tongue is so woefully inconsistent that a man who speaks eight languages may be a liar or slanderer in all eight.

The tongue never was designed to spill out bitter words, or even a mixture of bittersweet talk. The tongue was made to bless. Man is the only creature on the earth with the gift of speech. The cat mews, the dog barks, the bird warbles, the parrot repeats, the cow moos, the horse neighs, the pig squeals, and the sheep baas, but none of these can really speak. Only man has a highly developed voice box which permits articulate speech. What a perversion when this marvelous gift of God is prostituted to unholy purposes!

When a person accepts Christ as Saviour, redemption extends to his tongue as well as to his soul. Gradually, if not more rapidly, his speech should give evidence of the lordship of Christ. After James speaks of new birth and consequent new life, the next verse contains the command to be swift to hear and slow to speak (James 1:18-19).

The purpose of the preceding 11 chapters has been to bring the shortcomings of the tongue into clearer relief so that we shall be more alert to their subtlety and seriousness. This in turn should show us the need of constantly letting the Spirit of God mortify the deeds of this member of our body and control it for positive good.

But the tongue needs not only to be tamed, but also needs to be transformed into a fountain of constant blessing. For the tongue can bless as well as blast, heal as well as hurt, soothe as well as slander.

A FOUNTAIN OF BLESSINGS

The writer of Proverbs gives striking similes to drive home the blessings of speech. "The tongue of the just is as choice silver"

(Prov. 10:20). "Pleasant words are as an honeycomb, sweet to the soul, and health to the bones" (16:24). "A word fitly spoken is like apples of gold in pictures of silver" (25:11).

The Apostle Paul urges profitable use of the tongue. "Let your speech be always with grace, seasoned with salt" (Col. 4:6).

Here are some ways by which our tongues can be an uplifting influence:

AS AN INSTRUMENT OF EVANGELISM

For a person to believe in Christ he must hear about Christ. For someone to hear about Christ someone else must speak about Christ. These links in the logic of missionary strategy are emphasized in question form by Paul. "How shall they hear without a preacher?" (Rom. 10:14) And again, "Faith cometh by hearing, and hearing by the Word of God" (Rom. 10:17).

Some are converted through reading the Word, but most people need a spoken explanation to make the written Word clear. When an Ethiopian, riding along in his chariot and reading the Book of Isaiah, was asked if he understood what he was reading, he answered, "How can I, except some man should guide me?" (Acts 8:31) Most sobering is the thought that practically every person who is saved will be in heaven because someone used his voice to speak the Gospel. Not only is a presence required; so is a voice.

A wiretapper mixed up with syndicated crime sat near the back of the Billy Graham "canvas cathedral" in Los Angeles. Though Jim Vaus had heard this message often before, two statements especially impressed him. First was Graham's reminder, "What shall it profit a man, if he shall gain the whole world, and lose his own soul?" (Mark 8:36)

Up till then, cars, bank account, and other material things had been Vaus' ambition. Second, Graham's voice pierced through the tent: "There's a man in this tent who has heard this story many times before and who knows this is the decision he should make. This may be the last chance God will give him to decide for Christ." God used Graham's voice. Something inside Vaus broke, and he went forward to accept Christ. By "the foolishness of preaching" God saves people.

When Peter urged people to be saved on the Day of Pentecost, when the early church was scattered in all directions and went everywhere preaching the Gospel, when Paul in Christ's stead bade people be reconciled to God or persuaded them to flee the wrath to come, the instrument of speech was utilized. Paul often prayed that a door of utterance, to speak the Gospel, might be opened.

In dealing with non-Christians we are told to instruct these potential converts patiently and meekly, so that God will grant them repentance to the acknowledging of the truth. To the skeptic we are to be ready to give an answer relative to our faith. We are to contend for the Gospel against false teachers. Sound speech, along with an incorrupt life, can disarm unbelievers of some of their opposition to the Christian faith.

Countless thousands will be in heaven because of the witnessing tongue of faithful evangels—not only preachers and missionaries, but others who believed that their tongues must be employed in obedience to the Great Commission, which orders us to preach the Gospel to every creature. John Bunyan, author of *The Pilgrim's Progress,* was won to Christ through overhearing two women conversing about the love of God.

Speech is not only the instrument of instruction an evangelist uses, but it is also the means by which response is made to the Gospel. When faced with their sins, Joseph's brothers confessed their wrong in selling him into slavery. Likewise David, confronted by Nathan with his heinous double sin of adultery and murder, poured out his heart in genuine repentance. In order for one to be saved, his faith in Christ must be so deep that confession is made by the mouth to this belief (Rom. 10:9-10). Those who confess Christ before men will be confessed by Christ before His Father in heaven (Matt. 10:32).

AS AN INSTRUMENT OF EDIFICATION

After evangelizing our fellowmen we should help them advance in the Christian life. A word of instruction here and there will aid in their edification. The Great Commission bids us teach new disciples to observe Christ's commands. Prophesying, or speaking forth for God, provides a most beneficial outlet for the tongue.

Words are necessary to carry on the business of life. What a clumsy and tardy method of communication are paper and ink, compared with speaking face to face. The highest use of the tongue in the secular realm is probably teaching. He who teaches such subjects as history, science, and mathematics edifies by speech, for other truth exists besides biblical truth. However, he who teaches spiritual truth employs the tongue in a higher privilege. By words we can "edify one another" (1 Thes. 5:11).

The gifts of teacher, prophet, apostle, pastor, as well as evangelist, were given to the church to perfect the saints and edify the body of Christ. Church leaders were to be "apt to teach" (1 Tim. 3:2). Even as we lift our voices in singing psalms, hymns, and spiritual songs we teach one another.

A word of warning or reproof can often turn the steps of an immature Christian from paths of danger. A Christian young lady was beginning to keep steady company with an unsaved man. A trusted friend of the girl's asked, "Is he interested in spiritual matters?" The indirect admonition started the girl on a train of serious thought. The young lady, who loved the Lord deeply, realized that if she would marry her boyfriend, a major barrier would torment their relationship. In addition, she remembered the verse, "Be ye not unequally yoked together with unbelievers" (2 Cor. 6:14). She stopped dating him.

It's far better to build up than to burn down. Blessed are those who use their tongues for peacemaking.

When two women of the Philippian church, Euodias and Syntyche, were at odds, Paul urged them to be of the same mind in the Lord. He had preceded this by describing the lowly mind of Christ, which led Him down from the heights of glory to earth, where He humbled Himself by becoming a Man, a servant, and finally a victim of death, even the shameful death of the cross, which was reserved for slaves and criminals. In the face of Christ's condescension, how could these woman help but be reconciled to each other? Though Paul's words were in writing, they give us an idea of how he smoothed out difficult situations with spoken words.

AS AN INSTRUMENT OF ENCOURAGEMENT

A high school teacher found his class in noisy bedlam on entering the room. Slapping his open hand on the desk, he ordered loudly and sharply, "I demand pandemonium!"

The class quieted down immediately. The teacher commented to fellow teachers later, "It's not *what* you ask for; it's *how* you ask it."

Lives can be profoundly affected by the way information is communicated. Truth can be conveyed in such a way as to give hope to a person, or devastate him. Our words can lead to a challenge, or set the stage for a crushing defeat. As a patient was wheeled into the operating room for major surgery, he was thrown into a panic because a nurse was softly singing, "Nearer My God to Thee."

A Texas doctor tells of thoughtless words of health personnel which a surprising number of patients hear while supposedly under general anesthetic, such as, "I'm going to shoot him now," referring to an injection by needle. Or, "This just isn't my day." The patient worries, "Has he cut the wrong place? Has he stopped my air supply?" Too many, says this doctor, hurt patients by failing to watch their language. "If you cannot be reassuring," he advises his colleagues, "be quiet."

Advice should be stated positively. For example, instead of the negative, "Take one at mealtime for indigestion," the doctor could better suggest, "Take one at mealtime to improve your digestion."

Shakespeare spoke of words that were "razors to my wounded heart." Milton wrote of "apt words" with "power to suage [assuage] the tumors of a troubl'd mind."

The *American Journal of Nursing* (Jan. 1985) spoke of the healing power of hope which is so necessary to prevent the physical and mental deterioration that comes with the despair brought on by illness. However, it also pointed out that hope, which nurtures an individual's recovery, doesn't necessarily spring eternal, but often has to be carefully mined and channeled. "Caregivers have the power to be either 'dispiriting' or 'inspiriting' to their patients. The health care professional can intervene by using techniques designed to inspirit: assure the patient that he/she is loved, needed, and valued" (p. 23).

This same advice can be carried over into church congregations, Christian shepherding flocks, and small Bible study groups. Helpful advice can encourage those that need inspiration. Barnabas, whose name means "son of consolation," seemed always to be using his tongue to help. For example, when the apostles at Jerusalem were not quite convinced of the fact of Paul's conversion, Barnabas brought Paul to them and verbally recommended him.

The major portions of Paul's epistles, which are so helpful in written fashion, indicate how uplifting his personal speech must have been. His constant prodding of timid Timothy to be of strong mind gives an idea of how he always tried to bring out the best in people.

Chrysostom said, "Slander is worse than cannibalism." Instead of devouring one another, we should use our tongues to build each other up. How often people say, "I heard something said years ago, and I have never been able to get away from it." To challenge the best in someone is far better than tearing down. In the hour of sorrow the tongue can comfort. The sick, shut-in, and bereaved need the soothing balm of God's solace. For this consoling ministry God uses human voices that are yielded to Him.

Dr. George Sweeting, president of Moody Bible Institute, tells of a student who walked around campus with a cane. Just a few months before she planned to enter Moody, Amber learned she had cancer, which required major surgery on her leg, weeks in the hospital, and a series of chemotherapy treatments. Though pain was her constant companion, lying on her hospital bed she radiated a peace that attracted all she met. Her roommate was a frail two-year-old girl born with cancer. Though Amber could barely move, she would sit for hours with her little friend and read her stories. By noting Amber's response to her illness, plus her concern for their daughter, the little girl's entire family trusted Jesus as Saviour.

When Amber spent her summer at home in San Jose, California, she led a counseling ministry with hospital patients through her church. Also, the hospital where she received her treatment invited her to return, to help other young people cope with their illnesses. During the school term, as she made her way around the campus, she could often be seen stopping to encourage a classmate.

AS AN INSTRUMENT OF PRAYER

How often the Bible exhorts to prayer! Moses, David, Elijah, and thousands of Old Testament saints lifted up their voices to God. Our Saviour, Peter, Stephen, Paul, and all New Testament Christians spoke aloud with God. At least one noted Christian leader of our day prays audibly even in private devotions, for it forces him to concentrate and thus prevents mind-wandering. Public prayer, whether in a formal service or by the bedside of a sick one, has lifted spirits weighed down with cares.

There is much to pray for—that laborers will go forth into the harvest, that utterance may be given Christian workers, and prayer for those in authority. How little praying we do! We should pray with supplication, with thanksgiving, with faith, with forgiveness. Volumes have been written on prayer.

When we are tempted to criticize another, why not pray for him instead? If we feel like grumbling or becoming angry, why not lift our voices in prayer? In this way our lips will pour forth sweet instead of bitter words.

AS AN INSTRUMENT OF PRAISE

Appreciation should be expressed to others out of hearts grateful for kindnesses rendered. A thankful tongue can be a blessing in the circle in which we move. But above all others, praise should be ascribed to God.

Man was made to glorify God and to enjoy Him forever. Man never does wrong by praising God; in fact, he better fulfills his own destiny. God has given him a tongue with which to praise his Maker. Davidic psalms exalted God. The early church praised God. We should sing unto God with grace in our hearts. Someone has described praise as a combination of words plus a feeling of joy. Birds have only feeling as they sing, but no words. But to the human race has been given feeling and the ability to express itself in words. The highest faculty of speech is the praise of God.

Speech enables Christians to be prophets, priests, and kings, in a limited manner. As prophets we use our tongues to speak for God to the edification of others. As priests we offer not a lamb but the sacrifice of praise, the fruit of our lips. As kings we are superior to lower creatures by virtue of this royal faculty of speech.

CONCLUSION

The tongue is a remarkable organ. If we used our arms or legs as much as we used our tongues, we would be unbelievably stiff and sore. But tongues never tire, nor have we ever observed one with a sling or splint on it.

Artificial joints are used these days. Also, many organs are transplanted. But we have not yet heard of an artificial or transplanted tongue.

One day the heathen philosopher Xanthus was expecting friends for dinner. He ordered Aesop to provide the best things for his table that the market could afford. Only tongues were provided. The cook was ordered to serve these with different sauces. Course followed course—all tongues. "Did I not order you," said Xanthus in a violent passion, "to buy the best victuals the market afforded?"

"And have I not obeyed your orders?" answered Aesop. "Is not the tongue the bond of civil society? The organ of truth and reason? The instrument of our praise and adoration of the gods?"

On the morrow Xanthus ordered Aesop to go to the market again and buy the worst things he could find. Aesop again purchased nothing but tongues, which the cook was ordered to serve as before. "What—tongues again!" cried Xanthus.

"Most certainly," replied Aesop. "The tongue is surely the

worst thing in the world. It is the instrument of all strife and contention, the inventor of lawsuits, the source of division and wars; it is the organ of error, lies, of slander, of blasphemy!''

Only twice do the Gospels say that Jesus sighed. Once was when the Jews asked for a sign (Mark 8:12). The other was just before he loosed the tongue of a man with an impediment of speech. Mark wrote, "And looking up to heaven, He sighed, and saith unto him . . . Be opened. And straightway . . . the string of his tongue was loosed, and he spake plain" (Mark 7:34-35). Could the reason for Jesus' sigh have been the realization that He was about to confer on this creature the power of clear speech? Up to now the man had not had the power to sin or bless with his tongue. Henceforth this tremendous potential was his. It would be the medium of either powerful good or terrible evil. Jesus was saying in effect, "Son, hitherto you have been shut out from the power of sinning with your speech, but now you stand on the brink of awful responsibility. You have a tongue to use or abuse. From it may flow streams of sweetness or rivers of bitterness.''

Someday our tongues will be perfectly redeemed. In heaven there will be unimaginable praise to God the Father and God the Son. There will be those who rest not day or night, continually saying, "Holy, holy, holy, Lord God Amighty . . . Thou art worthy, O Lord, to receive glory and honor and power; for Thou hast created all things and for Thy pleasure they are and were created" (Rev. 4:8, 11).

And joining those voices will be a multitude of others, 10 thousand times 10 thousand, and thousands of thousands, saying with a loud voice, "Worthy is the Lamb that was slain to receive power, and riches, and wisdom, and strength, and honor, and glory, and blessing" (Rev. 5:12).

Then every creature in heaven, on the earth, and under the earth, and such as are in the sea will blend in saying, "Blessing, and honor, and glory, and power, be unto Him that sitteth upon the throne, and unto the Lamb forever and ever'' (Rev. 5:13).

Sometimes, in singing, we ask for a thousand tongues to sing our great Redeemer's praise. Till that day of realization we shall need constantly to use aright the one tongue we do possess, praying, "Take my lips and let them be filled with messages for Thee."

With the psalmist we say, "Let the words of my mouth, and the meditation of my heart, be acceptable in Thy sight, O Lord, my strength, and my Redeemer" (Ps. 19:14).